POSSIBILITY POND

A Story of Success Principles and Practices

Dr. George McMaster
Editor: Sandy McMaster
Artist: Albert Casson

Reciprocity Publishing, Canada

Possibility Pond: A Story of Success Principles and Practices

A young beaver embarks on a challenging journey to save his home and family, discovering along the way timeless principles for resilience and success. Billy Beaver's adventures reveal practical lessons that readers of any age can apply in daily life, making Possibility Pond both an engaging story and a guide for living with courage and optimism. The hardcover edition features George McMaster's original tale with Albert Casson's illustrations, while the paperback and ebook include a Learning Companion filled with questions, discussion prompts, and activities that encourage readers to retell the story in their own words and connect it to their own experiences.

For every generation and every journey, Possibility Pond is a heartwarming allegory that unlocks the secrets of a positive mindset. From the playground to the boardroom, this inspiring book helps children, parents, teachers, students, and business leaders alike turn life's challenges into triumphs. Dive in—and discover the possibilities!

Copyright © 2001-2025 by Dr. George McMaster. All rights reserved.

No portion of this book may be reproduced in any form without permission from the author or publisher, except as permitted by the Canadian Copyright Act with regard to fair dealing: short excerpts for the purpose of research, private study, criticism, review or news reporting.

Editor: Sandy McMaster, Artist: Albert Casson
Designer: Daniel Doherty, www.ReciprocityPublishing.com

Second edition: 2025-09-05

ISBN: 978-1-928114-63-5 (hardcover: story and illustrations only)
978-1-928114-28-4 (softcover: story, illustrations & Learning Companion)
978-1-928114-29-1 (ebook: story, illustrations & Learning Companion)

Citation: McMaster, Dr. George. 2025. *Possibility pond: A story of success principles and practices*. Victoria, BC: Reciprocity Publishing.

Please address comments, questions, suggestions and your Success Principle icons to the author: Dr. George McMaster: gemmcmaster@gmail.com

Order *Possibility Pond* from Amazon. Contact the author for bulk purchase.

Other Books by Dr. George McMaster and Master Coach, Vic Lindal:

EndPoint Vision and Beyond: Live your Preferred Future Now. 2013. Principles and practices for applying EndPoint Vision (EPV) in all areas of your life. Book, e-course, challenge game, AI self-coaching app, workshops and personal coaching available from www.endpointvision.com

Radical Coaching: Methods for Winning. 2014. A team training manual containing innovative coaching practices, linear ranking worksheets and resources.

To our grandchildren
Nolan, Nash, Logan, Hudson, Liam, Marlowe and Paige
and to all generations to come.

May Billy's journey inspire you to do your best and may
the ideas and principles help you live your best life.

Contents

Preface: The Importance of Stories for Learning — 8
    Why this book is valuable to you. — 8
    Overview of the Success Principles — 11
    The Learning Companion — 13

Possibility Pond
    Chapter 1: Opportunity Comes From Adversity — 16
    Chapter 2: Change is Coming — 18
    Chapter 3: Billy Chooses to Act — 20
    Chapter 4: Watching Out for Danger — 22
    Chapter 5: Obstacles on the Road to Success — 26
    Chapter 6: Billy Trusts His Intuition — 29
    Chapter 7: Advice from Unusual Sources — 33
    Chapter 8: Pushing Through Adversity — 36
    Chapter 9: Guarding Your Vision — 39
    Chapter 10: Finding Allies — 42
    Chapter 11: Asking at the Risk of Receiving — 46
    Chapter 12: There Has to be a Way — 49
    Chapter 13: Going the Extra Mile — 52
    Chapter 14: Finding Allies in Unusual Places — 56
    Chapter 15: Elder Speaks His Truth — 59
    Chapter 16: Changing Impossible to Possible — 62
    Chapter 17: The Gift of Being Calm — 65
    Chapter 18: Billy Trusts His Vision — 69
    Chapter 19: Leading by Example — 72
    Chapter 20: Staying Present During a Journey — 77
    Chapter 21: The Vision Becomes Reality — 81

APPENDIX

Believe (lyrics) — 85

20 Success Principles: Definitions and Tips for Remembering — 85

Template: Your Major Definite Purpose (MDP) — 88
    A. Define Your Major Definite Purpose — 88
    B. Accomplish Your MDP — 89

Applying Goal Setting to a Major Definite Purpose — 90

Success Stories — 92
    A. An Immigrant's Story — 92
    B. An Artist's Story — 92
    C. The Mastermind Alliance (MMA) — 93

The Role of This Book in Life's Journey — 95
    A. Attracting the Life You Would Love to Live — 95
    B. The Natural World Responds to Your Thoughts — 95
    C. The Power of Success Principles to Impact a Business — 96
    D. Inoculating Kids for Success — 97
    E. Two Stories: Do Thoughts Create Reality? — 98

Some Ideas on Helping Keep the Earth (and ourselves) Healthy — 100

A final key take-away from Possibility Pond: Adventurizing — 101

Acknowledgements — 103

About the Creators — 105

Success Principle Checklist/Log — 107

Praise for Possibility Pond

George brings considerable life experience to his work with Success Principles, having created a book that is truly accessible to all. I can attribute my success in such diverse careers as volleyball coach and personal coach for corporate executives, in part, to my ability to implement the many Success Principles clearly described in *Possibility Pond*. I have been able to use these concepts to guide my clients on the path of success.

My experience as an Olympic commentator for Volleyball required the ability to look at teams and individuals on a team, and discern why they have been successful or failed in their quest. Having the Success Principles at my fingertips meant that I could provide a deep and meaningful evaluation for the viewing audience.

In my opinion, many of the most accomplished individuals and organizations in the world owe their success to a deep understanding of the concepts that are given to the reader through this story. They are dissected and described clearly in the text providing immediate application through clear presentation. I believe that anyone, no matter what stage of life or career they find themselves in, can benefit immensely from studying, enjoying and sharing *Possibility Pond*.

-- Vic Lindal, Master Coach,
Volleyball Hall of Fame Inductee, Olympic volleyball
commentator, author, personal coach for greatness

I was fortunate to grow up with parents who supported active learning, personal initiative, discipline, taking action and learning from adversity and mistakes. They encouraged us through example and storytelling, to develop ourselves with purpose, toward an honourable, helpful and fulfilling life.

In George McMaster's book, *Possibility Pond*, I recognize so many of the principles that guided me through the ups and downs of life. His engaging story appeals to children and adults alike. He has masterfully crafted a practical guide for us to learn and teach Success Principles. After reading *Possibility Pond*, I am inspired to more mindfully apply Success Principles using the easily accessible framework described.

George's book has left me feeling better equipped to do as Elder suggests to Billy, "...help others dream their dreams. Encourage them to share their dreams and tell them to keep moving forward to make their dreams happen. Help them have faith in themselves."

-- Marcel Doré MD, Hospitalist Physician,
DDP Yoga Instructor, husband, father, grandfather,
entrepreneur, mentor and teacher

I am grateful to have parents who were interested in The Science of Success and had the vision to share it with their children. I'll never forget my dad coming home one day with the Napoleon Hill workbook and offering each of his four sons $500 cash to complete it. That was a lot of cash back then and a powerful motivator. When he presented a two-day seminar to his company on The Science of Success, we were there. Talk about belief and desire to impart these time tested values in your kids!

Throughout my life I have often been described as laid back and friendly. In the same breath many people also describe me as a dog with a bone. I have a deep well of determination to draw from that has helped me to thrive in the tumultuous and ever changing music industry. I was raised with the tenets, "Going the extra mile", and "Within every adversity is the seed of an equal or greater benefit, if you look". This foundation is something that I feel is bedrock in my psyche and I would have loved to have had *Possibility Pond* brought to my attention as a child, as I don't think you can start building that foundation too young.

I'm thankful for these teachings as I now have two young girls that I'll be able to start sharing the principles of success with in such a brilliant and animated way. The most powerful tool in communication is storytelling, especially with youth, where attention is at a premium. In my humble opinion, this book should be part of the national school curriculum. In school, we are taught math, language, art, physical education; this book incorporates the most important subject of them all: The Science of Success.

-- Luke McMaster, musician, performer, composer of the Possibility Pond song, "Believe"

George McMaster is an incredible human being and I am beyond grateful for his guidance and teachings as a young entrepreneur. I met George when I was 20 years old, running a College Pro Painting franchise and little did I know this meeting would forever change the trajectory of my life. George introduced me to the teachings of Napoleon Hill. George taught me how to manifest my desired reality by establishing a clear vision and priming my mind for success using the teachings from his books *End-Point Vision and Beyond* and *Possibility Pond*.

One year after meeting George I went on to win entrepreneur of the year with College Pro Painters that has over 100 franchises. I also started the company I am currently operating, Primitive Patterns, a health and wellness company dedicated to helping people become balanced in mind and body through unique health experiences. Without George's mentorship this would not have been possible. George's book, *Possibility Pond*, is jam packed full of lessons that anyone can draw wisdom from. I have used the exact principles in this book to manifest the reality I am now living. "Opportunity comes from adversity," and Define your Major Definite Purpose" are but two lessons you will find within this book that can change your life, and put you on the path to success in business and in your personal life.

-- Lucas Burrella, entrepreneur

Preface: The Importance of Stories for Learning

Why this book is valuable to you.

This book is about storytelling, its importance and, how it impacts our ability to connect with others and learn. It is designed in such a way that it can be read and then easily shared with others, such as a parent might do with their children. The reader comes to know the story and the concepts within it and then can readily share it in their own words. The story of **Billy Beaver** is a way for people of all ages and backgrounds to learn the Success Principles of Napoleon Hill and understand how to apply them within their lives. It opens the door for the reader to then share these teachings with family, friends, colleagues and one's community. Stories help us make sense of our world and inform us on how to live our best life.

> *"I would ask you to remember only this one thing. The stories people tell have a way of taking care of them. If stories come to you, care for them, and learn to give them away where they are needed. Sometimes a person needs a story more than food to stay alive. That is why we put these stories in each other's memory. This is how people care for themselves."* -- Badger speaking in *Crow and Weasel* by Barry Lopez

The ability to tell stories is a valuable success attribute to develop. It enables us to learn deeply, connect with others and to have shared understandings. Storytelling is an important skill for all of us and is a significant modality for parents to use to educate their children. Reading *Possibility Pond* puts you on the path to developing your storytelling skills. Once you have read it, share it with someone, turning the pages and allowing yourself to tell the story in your own words with the text and pictures as a guide. Adopting this approach will allow the concepts in the story to be internalized, remembered, and then put into practice and shared. The questions in each learning section can be used to deepen one's understanding of each success principle, making them easier to internalize and finally, allowing you to **tell the story in your own words**.

There is a wisdom that suggests working to improve our ability to communicate our thoughts and feelings with each other, to achieve understanding, is a critical skill. People have achieved success by doing just that. Expressing yourself clearly, sharing ideas with others allows you to retain the information. The *Possibility Pond* story contains many practical concepts, and if you are intent on remembering them or wish to communicate your understanding of the concepts, then I encourage you to share them with others often. When learning is not shared you will likely find it is difficult to retrieve the concepts when you need them. When you find a good story you want to remember and share with others, then retell it right away or your memory will fade. **Sharing with others will ensure that you never forget it.**

"It is better to give than to receive," is in action here. In order to retain the understanding of this or any other subject you happen to be studying, you must give it away to someone else. You must learn it, explain it, discuss it, and pass it along to others. If you fail to do this, and attempt to hang onto the information for yourself, you will forget some of the subtleties imbedded in the ideas. Lacking the ability to grasp the nuances of an idea may impact the level of your success later in life. Watch for ways I structure the story and associate materials to facilitate memory and successful application of the principles.

Sharing ideas verbally is only one modality. You can write stories based on experiences and learning that can be shared with others in your life. For example, writing a story with children that incorporates the Success Principles helps to bring the concepts to life. You can also illustrate the story using pictures of their faces and yours that you glue on stick figures, which brings the principles to life. Children love to see themselves making a difference in the world rather than only seeing others accomplish great things. By inserting one or more of the Success Principles into your stories they will gain understanding and learn what it looks like when they apply the principles to their own journey in the world.

After writing a story for and with my grandchildren in Ontario, their teacher asked me to come to class and share it. The class was enthralled and engaged, asking questions and participating in the re-enactment of the story. What a thrill for my grandchildren and me.

How I benefited from Success Principles

Using the Success Principles embedded in *Possibility Pond* allowed me to create this amazing life I live. My relationship with my wife and family has been enhanced by the use of these concepts. When I co-founded a home healthcare company, these principles formed the foundation that led us to success, becoming Canada's largest home healthcare company. Those who journeyed with me in the healthcare business experienced overwhelming success in the work place, in their home lives and in other areas as well. I introduced my four sons to the principles, feeling strongly that I was inoculating them for success. This led them to accomplish their goals in the diverse and challenging fields of psychiatry, investment advising and as a singer/song writer/music & documentary producer. Knowing these principles has assisted them in their success and allowed them to live the life that they chose. This lifetime of application permits me to make the bold statement that this book will benefit corporations, entrepreneurs, individuals, parents, grandparents, youth and anyone wishing to make positive change in their lives.

Our sons now have children and we are inoculating them so they can move through life in an empowered manner. Many have asked, "How did you balance work and family life?" Though the corporation was a huge success and demanded much of my time and energy, by transmitting Success Principles to my family, I remained close to my four boys, sharing a common language of success we could use to communicate. We now have a group text where everything is discussed, life's challenges along with life's joys, often basing our mutual support on the Success Principles. The boys and I meet for an annual weekend together, where we enjoy pickle-ball or golf and have the opportunity to share together. Our grandsons excitedly anticipate joining in once they are old enough. Our four sons love what my wife and I share with their children whenever we get together or care for them. Our care is steeped in and guided by the Success Principles.

It has been suggested that 30% of children today are being raised either wholly or partially by grandparents. This book can be used to assist grandparents in this task. When I see adults on their cell phones at a restaurant while with children, I am struck by the need to develop storytelling as a tool for building open communication and closeness with the children in their lives. This tool allows us to disconnect from the distractions of technology and reconnect in a direct and meaningful way.

It took much study and hard work for me to internalize Napoleon Hill's Success Principles, and then to transmit them to others in a powerful way. We live in a rapidly changing society and one that constantly demands more and more of our time. Fortunately, the latest research is clearly showing that an optimal way for remembering and deep learning in a timely manner is to share the ideas through stories. Evolution has wired our brains for storytelling therefore, it is worthwhile that we take advantage of this ability. A good story lights up much of our brains, including the parts that form memories.

The Power of Storytelling

Storytelling is also a fun way to learn. When teaching the ideas to corporations through story, the learning takes place rapidly and the ideas can be quickly implemented. Employees and leaders can then read the story to their families or work through it with their team and maintain congruence in all areas of their lives. Witnessing a CEO, his wife and daughter rush out in the hall during a session to celebrate and share an "Aha!" moment, led me to believe deeply in the process. Congruency has always been important in my life and rather than be a tough executive at work, then switch to a loving supportive father role at home, my desire was to have the same behaviour in both arenas. These principles allowed me to find that congruency.

This story, about a young beaver who faces challenges similar to those we all experience, demonstrates how easily Success Principles can be applied to our own lives. I felt it was especially important to use animals in the story to avoid the pitfall of identifying with human character shortcomings, which can lead to minimizing the message. The lessons presented in *Possibility Pond* are adaptable to all areas of life: personal, family, career and legacy. The beaver is easy to relate to as it is a family-centred creature who can change the earth's landscape in more powerful ways than any other animal, save humans, and they survive by making amazing adaptations. The reader can experience the highs and lows of the main characters and develop a sense of how Success Principles can be used to create change in their own lives.

Possibility Pond was written based on the principles of good storytelling to bring the material to life and demonstrate its effectiveness. What follows are the guidelines I used to build the story of *Possibility Pond*, ones you may wish to use when telling your own stories:

1. **The story must have struggles** and the listener/reader must be able to connect easily to the characters, relate to their plight, and be able to discuss the story long after hearing or reading it.

2. **It should be easy for the reader to imagine themselves** as the main characters by connecting to their actions and being able to relate to the narrative.

3. **Early conflict and growing tension keep the audience engaged** and invested in learning the outcome. The movie Titanic illustrates this well, when the hero and heroine attempt to find safety as the water rises steadily while the ship sinks. In *Possibility Pond* our hero, Billy, does not initially

succeed, rather he faces many different challenges on his journey before experiencing success.

4. **When conveying a story, one is challenged to draw the listener/reader in** and motivate them to discover the good news or the lesson, with possibly a surprise twist. A learning segment accompanies each significant point in *Possibility Pond*, which facilitates the opportunity for deep understanding. Questions are posed to assist in the reflection and internalization of the key ideas.

5. **Make your story interesting** to help your listener/reader form memories in many parts of their brain. Exciting portions light up the segments of the brain where emotions are found. By providing details of sight, smell, taste and sound the listener/reader's imagination is activated and those receptive parts of the brain also light up. On his journey, Billy envisions himself in *Possibility Pond* where he can taste the clear water, listen to the sound of waterfowl, smell the poplar buds, and look around at the virgin forest. This **Endpoint Vision** lights up the parts of our brains that receive these stimuli and connects us more deeply to the story.

When the story describes how Billy swims through the water, the motor cortex, the part of the brain responsible for movement, also lights up forming deeper memories. When the young beaver slaps his tail, you might clap your hands together, using sound to further stimulate your audience. To form memories, it is important that the listener/reader becomes a participant in the story, actively engaged through their senses and imagination, allowing them to connect to the story as their own.

The experience is shared in the memories of our listener/readers. An amazing outcome is that it's no longer our story; it's a shared experience that becomes their memory. I have written stories of experiences with our grandkids in which I take artistic license and embellish the details of our experience. What I have found interesting is, after time passes, they cannot tell whether the enhancement to the story actually took place or not. It is important to remember that we often cannot tell the difference between a real and an imagined event.

In addition to using the above guidelines to read the story, more ideas follow based on my experience, to help you expand your storytelling skills and deepen your learning of the principles. This story was designed to be transmitted over a variety of age groups and life stages, to have each of these groups deeply internalize the Success Principles and to make them their own. Younger children enjoy stories with a plot and action, while older children like stories with an interplay of characters. All ages enjoy rhythm, a strong, regular, repeated pattern of movement and events as the lead character approaches the objective. A story needs to be well paced with few slow or dull spots. We designed the *Possibility Pond* story to meet these criteria as the lead character proceeds to find a new home and create his environment.

If you are a parent or facilitator helping others learn through this story, then it will be helpful to do an initial read through to get the structure, and then read again thinking how you'd facilitate others' learning.

Great references on the internet include: *The Science of Storytelling: Why Telling a Story is the Most Powerful Way to Activate Our Brains*, and Uri Hasson's TED Talk: *This is Your Brain on Communication.*

The structure of *Possibility Pond*

First, some perspective: many psychologists believe that **you cannot think a thought unless you have the language**. I agree! Therefore, it is most important to learn the language of success. Ideas such as Major Definite Purpose (i.e. Something Significant Yet To Do, or Definiteness of Purpose) and Mastermind Alliance (i.e. a gathering of people who share your dream and can then help you achieve it), are a few of the critical principles presented in *Possibility Pond*. You will learn the language of success by reading and through telling the story. For example, understanding and appreciating the concept of Major Definite Purpose guided me to find an activity for my parents when they retired so that they could continue to live a passionate life.

This story also cautions you to be careful of the words you choose because we believe that **you become your language**. The river that Billy finds is named Impossibility Creek. A description can become an affirmation with the potential to limit your thinking. You will quickly discover how this name impacted the characters in the story. Our corporation name was We Care Home Health Services. 5500 or more employees went to work every day being reminded in a positive way, that caring and compassion are of absolute importance.

The book maximizes learning through storytelling and engagement. Each chapter comprises up to six parts:

- **Part 1: An Illustration** – if "a picture is worth a thousand words", an illustration will help you tell the story in your own words.
- **Part 2: The Story** - the text that conveys the challenges, actions and principles, and engages the reader/listener.
- **Part 3: Conversation Points** - an exploration of what was happening through a Success Principles lens. The perspective in this portion provides an insider explanation of what is happening to deepen the understanding and experience of the events as they unfold in the story.
- **Part 4: Learning Points** - where success principle concepts are used to describe what is taking place.
- **Part 5: Questions** - that invite the reader to reflect on what is being conveyed. It is said that most kids ask 350 questions a day, and the average adult asks 24. Questions expand our understanding through exploration and curiosity.
- **Part 6: Exercises** – to guide you to apply what you have learned and experience the Success Principles for yourself.

It is easy to see who might be learning the most. I have one grandson, Nash, who is amazing at asking questions. He thinks of diverse ideas which spark a network of many more possibilities I would never have considered. I am working on my ability to gently present methods to formulate possible answers, such as mind mapping. These days, an employee who is able to propose potential solutions to apparent challenges is a welcome asset to a business. Helping build skills toward this end is a delicate balancing act as one does not want to inhibit curiosity or the bringing forth of a problematic idea. I remember one dinner party where a guest was shocked at the challenging questions one of my sons, Jeff, was asking me. I thought they were legitimate, and did not stifle his curiosity.

How to maximize your learning

At first, focus on the story of *Possibility Pond*, reading it for pleasure. Then the Conversation Points, Learning Points, Questions and Activities are to be explored once the story is familiar. When you read the story, visualize it part by part. Become familiar with the illustrations in each chapter, and visualize how it would be for you. **An EndPoint Vision (EPV) is a vivid picture in your mind of what you want to achieve**, in this case, adopting the Success Principles into your life. By beginning your study with an initial read of the story you build your EndPoint Vision, facilitate deep learning and allow yourself to identify with the material. Research says, a story is the only way to activate parts of the brain so that a listener turns the story into their own idea and experience. This point is critical as the story is designed to model what we experience in real life and it demonstrates how we can successfully navigate adversities that we encounter. When you read or hear the story, you encounter the triumphs and adversities, and learn how to deal with them.

You have begun your practice! As Einstein says, "**In the middle of adversity comes opportunity.**" As you progress through the story, you will begin to practice the skills making them your own. You will find ease in applying these ideas to your own life, such as learning to switch from adversity to seeking the opportunity. It was thought that IQ was the most important trait for success. Later it was thought that EQ, Emotional Quotient, was most important. On reflecting what Success Principles has done for me, I would argue that **your Adversity Quotient (AQ) is your greatest indicator of success**, the ability to quickly transform adversity into opportunity.

Please think of *Possibility Pond* as a folk tale, one of the easiest stories to tell. It is simple, entertaining, and easy to understand. Peter Senge, in his bestselling book *The Fifth Discipline*, states that your success in life rests on creating good mental models or ways of thinking of things, such as metaphors.

Simple, clearly communicated stories stick with us and consequently, so will the Success Principles that are embedded in *Possibility Pond*. Keep it Simple, is a good guideline for you to adopt when sharing information, teaching or even making your case if you were presenting to a jury! The language, words, phrases and sentence structure have been expressed in a way that activates regions of the brain that make us truly relate to the events and experiences in the story. In the 5-star Netflix series *Bones*, the lead character is a brilliant forensic anthropologist. In one episode she makes a scintillating presentation to the jury; she is highly scientific but devoid of emotion. Although her evidence is correct, the case is lost. **The jury's brains were not lit up** as she told her story.

Overview of the Success Principles

Many thanks to Napoleon Hill who synthesized the ideas for achieving success into 17 essential principles. I added 3 additional principles that I believe are needed today: Determination, Persistence and Adaptability to Change (see the appendix). I would like to expand on this last principle about change.

Handling the Tides of Change

I added the 20th Success Principle, Ability to Adapt to Change, as the changes to our world and society have become exponential. Consider the Internet and expanding use of Artificial Intelligence. Their growth rate is extremely challenging for us to comprehend. To illustrate this rapid change, here is mental model to explore. Imagine there is a stream containing high levels of fertilizer flowing into a pond. Suppose that the weed cover doubles every day. The first day it might have 1% coverage, the next 2%, the next 4% and the next 8%. At this stage the change is not dramatic enough to cause any notice. At some point however, the pond becomes a quarter covered, the next day half, and to the shock of all, the pond is completely green the following day. Now the impact of fertilizer entering our natural water systems becomes real and scary. Many years ago I realized, **"Something is only as bad as your reaction to it."** This helped me respond to rapid change and reduce my stress level. Adopting this approach allowed me to pause and consider how to best respond to a situation, and then decide what action to take.

The story *Possibility Pond* helps restore a sense of meaning, which is so important if we are to successfully handle the tides of change. Without meaning or connection it is literally and metaphorically easier to go to sleep when faced with a challenge. In psychological terms, this is **learned helplessness**. This is something our mind does when the stimulation exceeds our ability to make sense of and absorb what is happening. We quietly give up attempting to learn or adapt because the stressors around us appear greater than our ability to handle them. While growing a large vegetable garden, I came close to experiencing that sense of helplessness when I encountered a prolific weed that generated an amazing number of seeds. It quickly took root and began choking out my crop. The solution was to work on the garden more frequently than I had anticipated. I learned that being aware of what was taking place in my garden at a much earlier stage in its growth would allow it to thrive with more ease. I needed to be aware of what was occurring around me to be successful in my gardening venture. Telling stories is one way of staying awake and aware.

It is comforting to note, when we enter a story, we relax and block out information irrelevant to what we are reading. Through the act of storytelling, we organize information into meaningful coherent patterns that capture our complete attention. A story such as *Possibility Pond* teaches us to **fight the tendency to go to sleep in adverse conditions**, in times of rapid change and when faced with a sense of overwhelm.

This is similar to the benefits that can be derived through meditation, which is an exceptional tool for being present and relieving stress. In his book *Navigating the Tides of Change*, David LaChapelle offers great perspective on how to react to rapid change.

The story of Billy Beaver maps out a journey required to accomplish something new, to change the old. **Handling these tides of change** and the associated uncertainty that we are all experiencing, I believe requires the set of guiding Success Principles presented in this book. Songbirds use the stars in the night sky to navigate during their migration around the globe. Like the stars, I believe that a form of the Success Principles, whether written down or passed on orally from generation to generation, have endured through all generations to help us deal with change. Internalizing these principles as a part of our core is important work for us all.

We appear to be in a period of chaos and confusion. If we go to solution, not to problem, we can understand that we are always on the edge of the new and possible. What's springing forth acts to remind us that reframing is an essential tool for how we create our world. By viewing what is happening with more kindness, electing to be kinder toward ourselves and others, we engage in the change process with less stress and more possibility. In moving toward order, the virtues of care and compassion are fundamental tools in addition to the guiding Success Principles.

I recently attended a funeral where the outpouring of love and honoring was effusive. It occurred to me that rather than reserving this depth of sharing about the passing of a life in a eulogy at a funeral, if we approach our day to day interactions honouring the people in our lives and expressing our love each day, it would make a difference in how our collective lives unfold.

A powerful idea: A vision, a Major Definite Purpose, or a sense of something significant yet to do, is essential as we move forward in life. This allows us to readily handle change. There are many things that we will experience as our lives unfold. What we think and how we behave ultimately affect what we will see and manifest. Awareness and internalization of Success Principles helps us clarify where we are going and what we will see. The vision we hold of the possible will carry us through the challenges and assist us in getting there. In the story of *Possibility Pond*, it is Billy's clear vision of the new pond that keeps him moving toward success and takes him through the trials of the present. Applying Success Principles will help you face your fear of the unknown. May this story help you find your own clear vision and path to success.

LEARNING COMPANION

The Learning Companion

Optimal learning comes from sharing ideas with others. Successful people are good storytellers. This page explains the Conversations Points, Learning Points, Questions and Exercises that are provided at the end of each chapter to help you build this skill.

Conversation Points
Review and discusses elements of the story.

Learning Points
Connect the story to the Success Principles.

Questions
Deepen understanding, anchor learning and remember the story by writing and sharing.

Exercises
Apply what you have learned, to make it your own. For example, retell the story in your own words, or draw your ideas using the picture as a guide.

Consider the idea of giving up ways you are living your life, that may cause difficulty, but are hard to give up.

Mind Mapping

Workspace: Write, reflect and discuss...
Use the lined workspace or a blank sheet to respond to the prompts in the Learning Companion. Consider using a journal to track your learning, log actions and observe results after applying the principles.

Notice Your "Aha!" Moments

During the gold rush, pioneers were searching for nuggets. Those who found them became wealthy. You will see the Knowledge Nugget icon in key places throughout this book. They indicate where we had an "Ah Ha!" moment while working with these ideas. We hope you have these too. Draw the icon in the margin and colour it GOLD when you are struck with an insight and then write it in your own words.

Visualization and concept mapping are powerful ways to make meaning, anchor learning and rehearse application. The brain stores new story elements and connects them to your existing knowledge, experience and values. You can represent this by drawing a mind map: Write the main idea in the centre. Add a branch for each topic, and then add sub-branches for related details. Keep it simple, a word or phrase per branch. Add icons to convey concepts.

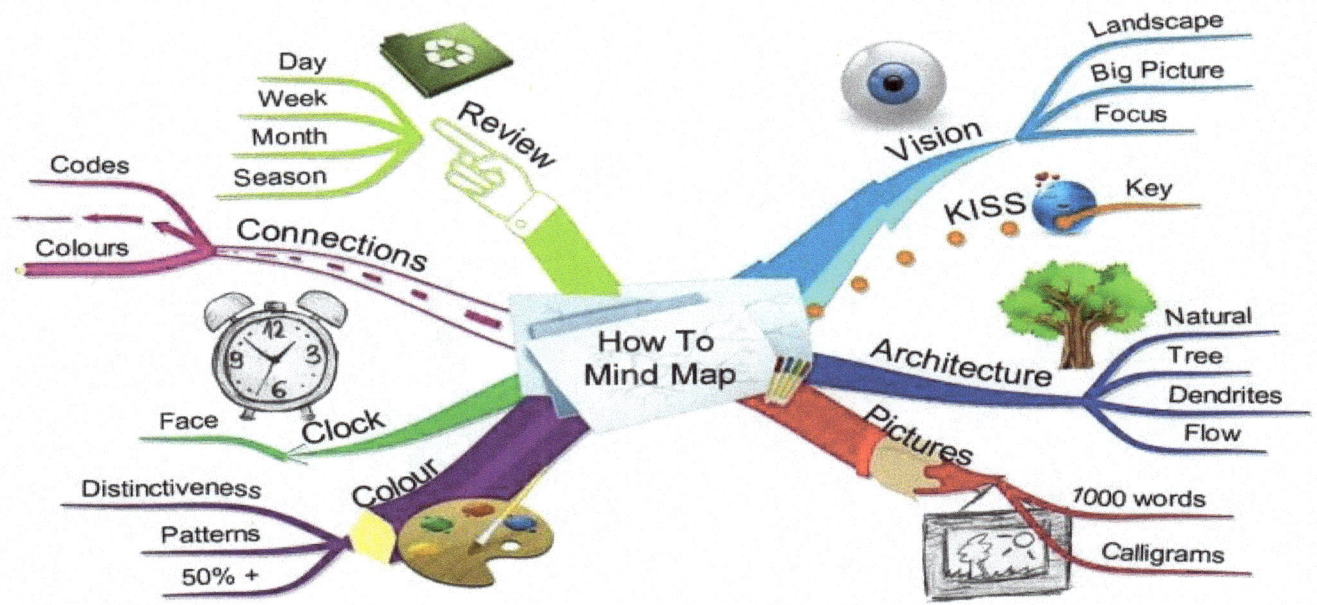

Image source: Wikimedia.org, Creative Commons Licence

Possibility Pond

POSSIBILITY POND

A Story of Success Principles and Practices

Dr. George McMaster

Editor: Sandy McMaster
Artist: Albert Casson

I'm going to get rid of you beavers once and for all.

Chapter 1: Opportunity Comes From Adversity

Farmer Ed and his dog, Yodel, roared down the dirt road in his old pick-up truck. As they came close to a beaver pond, the road was soft and slippery. Farmer Ed swung the wheel frantically trying to stay on the road, but the truck slid sideways, hit the ditch and came to a jolting stop.

Yodel was thrown onto the floor, and Farmer Ed banged his head on the window. They jumped out of the truck and ran toward the beaver dam. Farmer Ed, shaking his fist angrily, said, "I'm going to get rid of you beavers once and for all." Yodel joined in the threats by running back and forth near the dam, barking and growling at everything in sight. On his way back to the truck Farmer Ed grumbled to himself, "It's not fair, they're destroying my road!" It wasn't always this way in Happy Valley.

The beavers in this pond had only known a life of peace. "Why pick on us?" they wondered. "We have a right to be here too." Many beaver families had been calling this pond home for generations. Billy, a young valley beaver, lived with his parents and younger sister Chewie in a large lodge in the middle of a pond. It was made of mud and sticks packed tightly together. Years ago, his grandfather had dammed the stream that meandered through the valley, forming the pond that Billy and his family now lived in.

Farmer Ed lived nearby, raising cattle and growing hay in the valley fields. At first, his cows and horses loved to drink the clear water, but each year, Billy's family would fell the trees that were close to the water, and then build the dam higher to reach new trees. This raised the water level until it covered the hay and flowed onto the road, making it soft and slippery. The damage it caused made it difficult for Farmer Ed to tend his fields and drive to his home.

LEARNING COMPANION 1

Conversation Points: Adversity

This first part of the story demonstrates that both Farmer Ed and the beavers are facing **adversity**. Both parties could only see a problem, which limited their options. Thoughts like, "It's not fair." or "Why pick on us?" only served to deepen the negative experience and close the door on possibilities. Today more than ever, we need good affirmations to deal with challenges in our lives. Affirmations are positive expressions that guide our actions. To move from helpless to hopeful, Farmer Ed and the beavers would need to create some guiding affirmations. What our internal voice (self-talk) says to us is important, and being sure it is focused on helpful affirmations can make the difference between failure and success. "Within every adversity is the seed for equal or greater benefit" if you but look. This is a critical affirmation. It simply means that when something goes wrong, begin to look for the benefit or opportunity immediately, for there always is one. Do not waste any time being negative, or asking, "Why me?" for example. It could be that the universe is training you to accomplish a challenging goal in the future. Think of it as preparation.

Learning Points: Transmutation

Changing an adversity to an opportunity is a form of **transmutation**. When you can reframe any challenging situation into an opportunity, you are set up for success. For example, a person may be released from a job resulting in what may seem to be an upheaval. Forced to rethink their life goals, they end up doing something that they are passionate about instead. This book would be an excellent guide for their new journey. It is of vital importance in our lives to understand principles such as **Major Definite Purpose**, **Mastermind Alliance**, **Positive Mental Attitude** and **Go the Extra Mile**, concepts that will be explored as Billy's story progresses.

Questions

Framing questions is a critical ability that is useful to develop. Here are some questions to consider that will allow you to reflect more deeply on the teachings in this chapter. Answering these questions will form the basis for a productive discussion. Use the work space provided, a blank sheet or a journal.

- What adversity is Farmer Ed is facing?
- What benefit is this adversity to Farmer Ed? This is a good question if you are hanging onto an adversity.
- What adversities are Billy and his family facing? What could be the benefit to Billy and his family?
- What adversities have you faced in life?
- What has been the benefit of these adversities? There are always benefits, if you but look.
- Write down the affirmations that you currently live by. Are they serving you well?
- Did you relate to the idea of giving up some of the ways you are living your life? Some perspectives are challenging to change.

Exercises

- Retell the first chapter of the story in your own words, or draw your ideas, using the picture as a guide.
- An opportunity to write, reflect and discuss: See page 13 for more journaling ideas.

Successful people are storytellers.

Learning comes from sharing and discussing new ideas with others. Retell the first chapter of the story in your own words. Your ability to tell stories that facilitate learning will grow with every story you tell.

Possibility Pond

Each time Farmer Ed broke the dam, the beavers rebuilt it as good as new.

Chapter 2: Change is Coming

Each year Billy's family built their dam higher and higher. By doing this, the level of the water in the pond rose, making it easier for the beavers to reach the tender new poplar trees that they loved to eat. The extra water flowing into the pond surrounded Billy's den like a castle moat.

The water protected them from predators such as bears, wolves and coyotes who love to eat beavers whenever they can. Other wild animals, such as moose, muskrats, ducks, blue herons and geese would take advantage of the environment created by the beaver pond for food, shelter and water. The beavers were content and wished that Farmer Ed would just leave them alone. As the water rose higher in Happy Valley, there was more flooding in Farmer Ed's fields and less land for his cows to graze on. Routinely, Farmer Ed would break part of the dam in an attempt to drain the pond and save his pastures. He quickly discovered a beaver dam is difficult for anyone to tear apart. The mud and sticks are packed together so tightly they are as strong as concrete.

Each time Farmer Ed destroyed the dam, the beavers in Billy's colony would watch—their eyes poking out of the water like those of big scary crocodiles. As soon as Ed left, Billy and his family would start plugging the holes. By the next morning the dam would be as good as new.

Each time this happened, Farmer Ed became angrier and angrier. He renewed his vow to get rid of the beavers once and for all.

LEARNING COMPANION 2

Conversation Points: Determination

At this point in the story, it is obvious that Billy's family and Farmer Ed are caught in a conflict that they are both sustaining by their refusal to try something different. Farmer Ed has not taken more drastic action to get rid of the beavers yet and the beavers have not taken action to relocate. One of the most common roadblocks to success is procrastination, the delay of taking action toward a goal. Both Farmer Ed and the beavers are putting off taking alternative steps toward a more positive outcome. "You can always change something; it's darn hard to change nothing." These words reflect the idea of taking action, any action, as you can always change it. However, the action you take must be in the form of something not yet attempted.

Farmer Ed and the beavers are caught in a rut. They continue to apply the same solution to the problem, always getting the same results. **Determination** is an important attribute for success; however your efforts need to be intelligently considered. As a child, I remember going into an old shed on my grandmother's farm and finding a pile of dead flies on the window ledge. They had tried to escape the room through the closed window and after many hours of trying to go through the glass they would drop to the sill exhausted. After resting for a moment, they would pick themselves up again and buzz against the same hard surface, eventually dying. Freedom was an open door just a few feet in the opposite direction, all they had to do was turn 180 degrees and fly away, yet they continued to do what obviously didn't work. Why? And why are Farmer Ed and the beavers continuing to do the same thing? What else could they try? From this comes a great affirmation that provides guidance toward positive action: "If you always do what you've always done, you'll always get what you always got." Remembering this saying motivates one to seek other options.

Learning Points: Purpose

Often, solving our challenges requires imagination and innovation. Some call this creative thinking, critical thinking or thinking outside the box, which suggests coming up with a solution we haven't already tried. We must be able to step back from our situation and look for options that may seem impossible at the time. In the story, the beavers think the problem is Farmer Ed. They have become focused on one definition of their problem. A way to get a different perspective is to re-define the problem. Often, when people re-define their problems they come up with solutions that stimulate right action. As you will see, Billy re-defines the problem and comes up with a unique solution that becomes his **Major Definite Purpose**. A Major Definite Purpose is a goal you have identified that you are passionate about achieving in your life. It could take the form of a particular career, a high school or university degree or it may be as simple as building a clubhouse as a child. Often taking action to solve a problem, even if you don't know what the entire solution is, causes you to see an answer and can clarify or lead you to your Major Definite Purpose. Take action! If you are particularly stuck in coming up with a solution, you might use the Chinese proverb, "Reverse the obvious". That is, come up with all the ways you can think of to not make it work. In doing so, you will bring fresh thinking to the problem, and the right approach will often come to you.

Questions for Applying Success Principles

- Can you think of a time when you tried something over and over that didn't work, only to experience failure again and again? Share this time with someone.

- What "turn and fly away" experiences have you had?

- Can you think of a time in your life when you procrastinated to avoid doing something different to solve a challenge? An action could be as simple as replacing a burned out light bulb.

- What happened when you finally took action?

- What goal was achieved when you took action?

Exercises

We are wired to a way of being. Remember, repetition is the mother of learning. This idea will be voiced repeatedly in the text, and you will be encouraged to repeat learning activities.

- Make a list of your Major Definite Purposes past, present and future, and share them with someone supportive.

- Practice storytelling: Retell this chapter of the story in your own words. Sharing stories is the best way to internalize new learning.

"A tale is but half told when only one person tells it." — *Brett Popplewell*

Encourage others to tell the tale of *Possibility Pond* back to you and to their friends.

Possibility Pond

Billy protected Chewie from an angry beaver after she felled a tree that spanked him on his tail.

Chapter 3: Billy Chooses to Act

Today is Billy's second birthday. He is celebrating it with his younger sister, Chewie, who he has helped care for during the last year. Billy stayed with Chewie when his parents left the lodge to cut trees for food, to repair the lodge and to make the dam higher and stronger.

His parents didn't have more beaver cubs, as food was becoming scarce due to the constant battles with Farmer Ed.

Chewie was given her name because of her habit of chewing everything in sight, even the legs on her bed. Her parents didn't mind because beaver teeth grow a little each day, and the only way to keep them trimmed is through constant chewing. Billy loved his good-natured sister and whenever she got into trouble Billy was there to help.

One day, Chewie chewed a tree through. As it fell, it spanked another beaver on the tail sending him running frantically for shelter. When the beaver figured out what happened he turned and chased after Chewie, who ran to Billy for protection. Billy loved his role as Chewie's older brother.

Although Billy was happy with his role as a two-year-old beaver, it is customary for a beaver to leave home at this age. A young beaver is expected to set out alone to find a new stream or pond to call their own.

Billy had been feeling the urge to begin his search for some time now. He knew his journey would be risky. Even though he was young and small, at two years old Billy was strong enough to create a pond where none existed before. No other animal on earth has the power of a beaver to change the landscape, except man. In the water, Billy was safe due to his superior swimming skill but, when on land, Billy knew he was easy prey for bear and wolves. His journey had to be on land, and he was scared.

LEARNING COMPANION 3

Conversation Points: Risk

At this point, Billy finds himself faced with many challenges. Although his search instinct is part of a beaver's survival mechanism, when a beaver is two years old, the other beavers in the den will drive him out. Finding a new body of water became Billy's Major Definite Purpose--something significant yet to do.

Another adversity for Billy is the fact that he will most likely have to travel across land to find his new home, making him easy prey for a bear or wolf. As a water-based mammal, he is more agile in water than on land.

Yet, any new venture has some element of risk in it. Billy must decide if he wants to venture far to look for a new home or, stay close by and still be on Farmer Ed's property.

Embarking on any new venture often requires **risk taking**. Most great successes are the result of dealing with some adversity in a creative manner. Coco Channel, the founder of the Channel brand of fashion, fragrance and beauty products, reigned over the Paris high fashion world for most of the 20th century. She said, "My fortune is built on an idea that came from an old jersey that I put on because I was cold. I cut the front so that I wouldn't have to pull it over my head." Coco was an orphan and her only training was as a seamstress. Thus, after she cut the neck of her traditional jersey, she added a collar, ribbon and a knot to produce a Channel original...creating a fashion coup and the start of an empire.

Learning Points: Action

Coco Channel took an adversity and, with an idea, changed the world of fashion. Many ideas have their roots in adversity and their success in action. An idea will stay just an idea without action. Most often it is procrastination, the someday-I'll-get-around-to-it approach that is the greatest block to success. Tom Peters, author of the best-selling book, *Passion for Excellence*, said the way to approach action is, "Ready, Fire, Aim." stressing the importance of action, the firing. Paralysis by analysis can hinder problem solving; you keep aiming without firing. Nike, the running shoe company, has as its tag line, "Just Do It!" which is yet another reminder of the importance of action. Often when faced with adversity, taking action, any action, will ensure your progress, while you learn those things needed to attain your goal. This idea is also an amazing problem solving technique.

Questions

- What would you do if you were Billy? Would you look for a new place close to home or far away?
- What challenges do you face that require risk?
- What actions are you procrastinating about now?
- What ideas are you not taking action on?
- What are some of your blocks to action?

Exercise

- Practice Storytelling: Retell this chapter in your own words; write or draw additional ideas.

When Billy thinks about setting off to find a new home for himself and the other beavers, it seems like it is too big of a challenge. By embarking on this journey, Billy will learn that he is more able to accomplish this goal—and others—than he can imagine. As the story unfolds, watch for Billy to come to this realization. I learned this when training to hold my breath to improve my capacity for swimming under water…1, 1.5, 2, 2.5…3 minutes! 3.5 minutes seemed impossible to me, but the instructor said, "You are more capable than you can imagine." And he was right; I ended up doing four minutes.

Billy will learn this valuable life skill on his journey. Every child should have a similar challenge, one that thrusts them down a path they don't think they can ever reach the end of. They do so for the love of themselves and other people in the world. When they come to that destination, they will realize, as Billy did, that even the impossible can be accomplished, if you are but willing to take the first step and give it everything you've got. Then when you do succeed, you'll know that you can do anything you believe in and put your mind to.

Note: The song "Believe" that accompanies this book is a great reinforcement for the value of believing in a task or journey. The lyrics can be found in the appendix.

"Many people die at 30 and are not buried until they are 85." –*various authors*

Billy's story encourages us to take adventures throughout life. Live on the risk curve. Intentionally take risks so you are not on your death bed at 85 wishing you had done more.

Possibility Pond

As Billy crawled up a hill behind Happy Valley, he started to hear a voice in his head he'd never noticed before.

Chapter 4: Watching Out for Danger

Early the next morning, as the sun broke over the hills, Billy set off to search for a new home. He crawled out of his Happy Valley pond and onto the surrounding farmland. In the distance Yodel barked. Billy turned his head toward the sound, whiskers quivering in anticipation of his journey.

Before Billy went to bed he had heard the other beavers in his den talking about the previous night's hard work. They spent hours patching the holes Farmer Ed cut in the dam earlier that day. Billy sighed to himself as he climbed out of the pond, "I don't want to do the same thing over and over. I will find a new place to make my home that doesn't have people on it."

Billy turned away from the safety of his home pond and started his journey. He didn't know where he was going, but now he had a definite purpose, to find a new home far away from people like Farmer Ed. As Billy crawled up a hill behind Happy Valley, he started to hear a voice in his head he'd never noticed before. This voice scared him as it reminded him of all the dangers he faced. It said, "What if a bear eats you?" "Why are you leaving the safety of your home?" "Where are you going?" "You don't really know, do you?" "Why can't you be like the rest of the beavers and find a stream close to the dam?" "You can't find a new stream to dam."

"All the streams have already been found." The voice went on and on, almost sounding like his loving parents' last warning before he left home, "Watch out for danger!" As he listened to this voice Billy could feel his heart go thump, thump, thump. Finally, to overcome his fear, he decided to call this voice Egor. Billy worked hard to ignore the unnecessary doubt and fear Egor was trying to plant in his mind.

Once he quieted Egor, Billy continued on his way, travelling through the dark forest that lined the hills of Happy Valley. He followed a slender, winding path made by the deer. After a long time he noticed that he didn't smell water. Billy was thirsty, and as his heart thumped faster, Egor started in again with his doubtful words. "There isn't any water here. You should just go home!" Billy struggled with Egor and then finally decided to trust his instincts.

He proclaimed to himself, "I know there is a stream out there somewhere that can be dammed without causing problems for humans, and I'm going to find it!"

The voice in Billy's head went on and on…

"I have had a great many adversities, most of which never happened." – Mark Twain.

Notice Egor, the voice in Billy's head, is always coming up with challenges for Billy to deal with. For example, "You might see a snake!", which is a concern that would slow him down. Instead he can sideline that concern and only needs to deal with a snake if one appears.

Repeating the same action and expecting different results is the definition of delusion.

Possibility Pond

LEARNING COMPANION 4

Conversation Points: Ego Responding (Egor)

When Billy set off to find a new stream, everyone warned him of the dangers he might encounter. Doing something new can involve danger of some sort and it most certainly involves taking risks. New activities require you to get outside your comfort zone. The challenge is to meet these risks without feeding the fear. When you don't feed the fear, you are free to overcome both negative people and the internal voice of doubt. Billy called his **Egor**, which is short for **Ego Responding**. At this point in the story, Billy's biggest challenge is to control his mind and not let Egor sabotage his efforts. He cannot let negative thoughts overwhelm him on his journey and he must stay focused on his Major Definite Purpose: creating a new home for the other beavers and himself.

By clearing his mind of fear and doubt, Billy can be present in his environment and look for clues on his quest for a new stream. He will be able to recognize opportunities that present themselves as he moves over the land. If Billy becomes paralyzed by Egor's chatter he will miss the clues provided by his surroundings because his mind will be focused on fear and doubt. He will also limit possible contributions from Infinite Intelligence, the intelligence that quantum physics identifies in the universe.

It is important to note that Billy has clearly defined his Major Definite Purpose, or something significant yet to do, which is, "There is a stream out there away from humans and I'm going to find it!" In your endeavor to accomplish a goal, it is important to clearly define that goal, and to do it in 10 words or less, so that it can be remembered as a single thought bite and shared readily with others. This is often referred to as a **mission statement**.

Questions

- Do you have a voice in your head that gives you doubts and fears like Egor does to Billy?

- Are you able to keep your mind focused on your MDP or do you let doubts and fears paralyze you? Meditation is an excellent mind-conditioner to improve focus.

Exercises

- Write down all the reasons why you should be successful in achieving your own MDP. If you find it easier to list the reasons you won't be successful, you are with the majority of people. Consider this: do you have any fears that are just False Expectations Appearing Real (FEAR).

- Summarize Billy's mission statement in 10 words or less.

- Summarize your own mission statement in 10 words or less.

The accompanying questions and exercises mention that people easily come up with reasons an MDP is not achievable. Surprisingly, this can spur new ideas, making this a useful problem-solving technique. Use space below to capture any new ideas you may have.

Write, reflect and discuss...

_____
_____
_____
_____
_____
_____
_____
_____
_____
_____
_____
_____
_____
_____

Knowledge Nugget!

"Time matters most when time is running out." – *from the movie* Edie

When one dream becomes real, then it is possible they all can. That feeling does not stop at any age. It continues as long as we draw a breath. The movie *Edie* reinforces this thought in a wonderful, heart-warming way. The movie also reinforces the preciousness of time--a good lesson to learn at a young age.

Learning Points: Affirmations

Napoleon Hill observed that successful people make up their minds quickly, once they have enough information, and seldom change their minds. Unsuccessful people take a long time to make up their minds and change their decisions often. Once Billy started on his journey he immediately launched into action on his Major Definite Purpose, to look for a pond without people close by. He also found himself having to control his mind to keep his voice of fear and doubt, Egor, in check. This effort demonstrates another important element of success. The fact is, the only thing we have complete control over is our own mind. Billy fights to control his mind, full of inner doubts and fears, reasons he won't succeed, and why he should quit. Repeating his Major Definite Purpose as an affirmation is an important step in creating positive self-talk and a positive mental attitude.

Fear can be defined as **F**alse **E**xpectations **A**ppearing **R**eal. It is said that 95% of our fears never materialize, so they really are false expectations that may feel real. They are thoughts that need to be replaced by positive affirmations. Having a Major Definite Purpose (MDP), which is a positive affirmation, is one way to keep your mind fixed on a positive idea, instead of fears and doubts. Billy has clearly defined his MDP. With this firmly in his mind, he is able to quell the fears Egor keeps trying to distract him with.

9/11 Principle

Use the 9/11 principle to condition or program your mind for success. Write down your 9 positive qualities. Then write down the 11 reasons why you will be successful. Repeat the 9 out loud to yourself for 5 minutes in the morning, and repeat the 11 reasons for 5 minutes before retiring. Do this exercise for 91 days; if you miss a day, start over.

Here's a great example of a positive affirmation, "**The best do what the rest are not prepared to do**". It is saying, be your best. This exercise will re-educate your Egor, develop positive self-talk and teach you to control your mind. Write these two lists now. You may find generating the 9/11 to be a difficult task. Later in this book we will give you **20 Success Principles** to learn, which will provide suggestions for your 9/11 list. Working on your own now to create these lists will make the principles much more memorable when we give them to you.

Note: The 9/11 event in New York was an unspeakable tragedy. Using it in this way allows us to constructively reframe a catastrophe, facilitating transmutation, that is, changing it to something positive.

Exercise

- Retell this chapter of the story in your own words. Sharing stories is one of the best ways to learn and generate the desire for new knowledge.

- Consider how you could apply the ideas in the story, to your personal life, your family life and your career.

- A good practice is to write down key ideas as they pop into your mind, and then weave them into a story.

- In the space below, in your journal or on a separate piece of paper, list the following:

<u>9 Positive Qualities</u>   <u>11 Reasons for Success</u>

_____

_____

_____

_____

_____

_____

_____

_____

_____

_____

_____

_____

_____

_____

_____

_____

_____

_____

_____

_____

"The owl knows where you are and will swoop down to eat you," said Egor

Chapter 5: Obstacles on the Road to Success

After walking for hours without finding water, Billy felt thirsty, tired and scared. Alone in the forest near nightfall, he decided to look for shelter. He felt helpless because he was easy prey for many ferocious animals. Around him were dark towering trees rocking in the gusting wind.

The trees looked as though a huge bear was cuffing them with a paw, a habit bears have of scratching trees that makes them sway ominously. Billy turned and saw the large stump of an old tree that had been hit by lightning. The searing heat of the lightning bolt had burnt a cave into the base of the trunk. "This is a perfect place to rest for the night," Billy thought.

Billy was so tired he could barely crawl into the cave and lie down. As he dragged himself inside, he jumped up alarmed at the sound of an owl hooting nearby. Billy's eyes opened wide with fear. Egor started in once again, "The owl knows where you are and will swoop down and eat you." Immediately Billy recognized the voice of Egor and thought, "No, surely a mouse would be tastier than me."

He continued to crawl quickly into the cave and made himself comfortable. As Billy settled into the cave for the night, he was comforted by his vision of a cool stream where he would make a new home. Just as he was about to close his eyes, he sensed a movement in a corner of the cave. Egor said, "The owl has spotted you and if you leave the cave, he'll eat you for dinner." Instead of becoming scared, Billy decided to be happy that he made it this far. He said to himself, "I'm thankful that I've found this cave, and will be warm and safe tonight."

Nevertheless, as he said this, Billy looked nervously around the cave in the moonlight, hoping there was no creature in there with him, but there was!

LEARNING COMPANION 5

Conversation Points: Obstacles

On the way to achieving an MDP, there may be many possible obstacles to overcome. Success requires determination, as one never really exactly knows how far one must travel to reach a goal or how much time it will take. At this point in the story, Billy really doesn't know the distance he will have to travel to find his new home. It may be a short distance away, or it may take him many more days to reach it. He must continue with **faith**, the belief that he can reach his goal. At times like this, it often helps to have a group of supporters behind your efforts that believe in your goal. Billy does not have the support of a group at this point. He is reliant upon himself to stay motivated about his goal. Except for Egor, he is alone in his quest for a new home. What he does have is belief in himself and gratitude for his progress, abilities that keep him positive instead of fearful as he retires for the night. To Keep Moving Forward (KMF) toward success, Billy must make Egor into an ally. This is most important, a Mastermind Alliance with himself.

Learning Points: Mastermind Alliance

In proceeding toward any MDP, it is helpful to have what is called a Mastermind Alliance (MMA). An MMA is a group of people who believe in your goal, where no discord enters as they assist you, and who support you unconditionally in your quest to reach it. An MMA is different from a team in that members of your MMA believe in your MDP. MMA members are there for emotional, intellectual, physical and spiritual support. They are people who believe in you, and will encourage and assist you to press on when you are faced with blocks along the path toward your goal. A good MMA is made up of people who meet with you regularly during your quest and who provide knowledge, guidance and energy to help you achieve your goal. An MMA helps lessen the fear of uncertainty.

Questions

- What are the obstacles Billy is facing?

- Do you have a Mastermind Alliance for a current goal you have? Who is in it?

- You are the average of the five people who you are closest to. Give each person a score out of 5, Where 1 is low contribution, and 5 is exemplary contribution.
  Person #1 ____, #2____, #3 ____, #4 ____, #5 ____
  Add up the total and then divide by 5.
  What is the average score? _____

- Have you ever had an MMA for a goal you wished to accomplish? Who were your allies?

- Do you have family members or friends who tend not to be supportive of your goals and ideas? Who?

Write, reflect and discuss...

Knowledge Nugget!

Keep Moving Forward (KMF)

You'll always encounter negative input from your Egor or other people. Listen for valid points that may be made, adjust if needed and then proceed. Keep Moving Forward (KMF) is a critical problem-solving tool. Staying positive, that is, having a positive mental attitude, is one of the most beneficial Success Principles. It is key to longevity—living a long and healthy life. Work at understanding Success Principles in order to give yourself the ability to create positive change.

The author is sheltered by a tree on Vancouver Island that was struck by lightning. He did not spend the night in it, and fortunately, there were no webs nor Willy the Spider inside. However, he had heightened awareness, as Billy must have felt. A little fear?

Possibility Pond

A recommended guideline for meeting with your MMA is to establish **a set time, a set place and a set agenda.** Knowing that your Mastermind Alliance is there for you and ready to help will give you strength.

One interesting fact about a Mastermind Alliance is that sometimes your immediate family cannot be a part of it. Some family members may be over-protective and not want to see you fail. The result is that they may advise against a risk that is necessary to succeed. Siblings may be envious of your efforts toward success and may not support you, to protect themselves. Even with an MMA, you must assume full responsibility for your journey. Billy does not have an MMA at this point.

A great affirmation is, "If it is to be, then it is up to me." Gratitude is also an important element to success. Developing a Gratitude Complex, the ability to be thankful for the gifts of each day, is a good way to stay positive and defeat your Egor. Billy acknowledges his safe shelter for the night thereby practicing his gratitude complex. Your success is enhanced by the gratitude you offer daily.

Questions

- Do you have a Gratitude Complex? Do you go to bed each night by reviewing what you are thankful for that day?
  __Daily; __ Sometimes; __ Seldom; __Never

- What are you thankful for today?

- What activities and adventures from yesterday are you thankful for?

- What will you be thankful for tomorrow?

Exercises

- Retell this chapter of the story in your own words. Sharing stories and experiencing others' reactions deepens your understanding and helps you internalize the concepts. You will also improve your ability to tell stories in general.

- Summarize insights you have had from the story so far.

- Gather material that gives further insights into the story, such as the book, Think and Grow Rich, by Napoleon Hill. Note the word 'rich'; it can mean much more than monetary reward; it can for example, mean having good friends or a pleasant personality.

Write, reflect and discuss…

Knowledge Nugget!

Exercise Your Freedom of Imagination!

When Billy pursued his desire to save the beaver colony from farmer Ed, his parents were reluctant. However, he was given the freedom to be an adventurer, and believe what he chose--that there was a stream somewhere out there that could save them. This freedom of imagination and spirit (defined as having the qualities of courage, energy and determination), are I believe, two of the most valuable things a beaver (or person) can possess. In addition, having the freedom to think what you want is critical.

Billy was still afraid, but he watched with interest as the spider worked.

Chapter 6: Billy Trusts His Intuition

Billy scrambled to the back of the cave and tried to make himself invisible. He slowly peeked over his shoulder. He didn't see an owl, but he did see something else. Billy cautiously looked closer. He could just make out the shape of a huge, hairy spider shooting out a silk thread.

He sighed with relief and wondered what the spider was doing. Just then a gust of wind blew the long, sticky thread at his face. Billy ducked and the thread swung to the other side of the cave opening and stuck like an octopus's sucker. Then the spider scurried along the thread on its eight hairy legs, using this new anchor line as support for its new web. In this way, the spider was easily able to bridge the gap in the cave opening and began to weave an elaborate round web using this support. Billy was still a little afraid, but he watched with interest and curiosity as the spider worked. In a few minutes a beautiful web had formed. "So that's how a spider creates a web," Billy whispered to himself. "First it secures a bridge across the opening where it wants the web to be and then…"

The sound of Billy's voice startled the busy spider who stopped working and looked at him quizzically, "Who are you and what are you doing in here?" it asked. "I've never seen anything as funny looking. Your huge tail is as big as you are, and those long, buck teeth, well, you certainly are not as attractive as us spiders!" Billy hesitantly introduced himself, "I'm Billy Beaver and I'm looking for a stream to make a new home. Who are you?" "I'm Willy the spider. When people see me they're usually afraid and they say they get the willies" it explained in a voice of clicking sounds. While Willy was talking, a large bug landed on the web and became trapped. Willy scurried over and wrapped the bug in silk thread, like an Egyptian mummy. The bug wasn't getting away. Billy was only too happy that Willy preferred bugs to beavers.

Possibility Pond

LEARNING COMPANION 6

Conversation Points: Choice

Billy continues to face challenges on his journey and how he responds to these challenges will determine his success. He is a little beaver, far from home and the safety of water, and he is encountering tremendous uncertainty. Consider how it might feel as a little beaver trapped in a cave with a huge spider and hearing the howl of wolves and the hoot of hunting owls in the night.

Heading home might seem like a great option. How Billy reacts now will determine his success. If he keeps his mind focused on his immediate experiences, instead of letting Egor run around his mind like a pack of jumping monkeys, he has a chance.

His greatest Mastermind Alliance at this point in the story is himself and how he chooses to work with Egor. Billy has done a great job of controlling Egor up to this point and now needs to train him to be more supportive.

Using affirmations is one way, where you repeat a word or phrase often, and then it becomes part of you. For example, I regularly introduce myself as Curious George the monkey. And scratch both armpits. People laugh and remember my name. When I'm deciding whether to do something, my inner Egor sometimes says, "Of course you will; you're Curious George." This is the power of affirmation.

Learning Points: Belief

Even though Billy faces adversity, he is still confident in achieving his MDP. Despite the obstacles, Billy still believes he can find a new home without humans.

There is a famous saying by Napoleon Hill about ideas such as Billy's, "Whatever the mind can conceive and believe, it is possible to achieve." The most famous example of the application of this expression can be found when we consider Thomas Edison and the development of the light bulb. Edison conceived of the idea of a light bulb and then he believed, or knew, he could design one. After 10,000 unsuccessful experiments, he never lost faith. Some people might call them failures. However, he looked upon the experiments that didn't work as the process of elimination. He reframed them as successful steps. For Edison, each so-called failure meant he had eliminated one more idea that didn't work.

Questions

- Can you think of ways to control your mind when you face adversity? Brainstorm answers with others.
- Rephrase the statement, "Whatever the mind can conceive and believe, it is possible to achieve." How are your personal affirmations helping you achieve your goals?

Write, reflect and discuss...

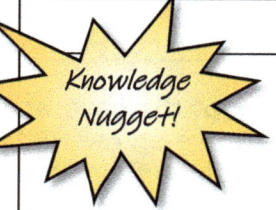

Repeat the words, "Cancel, Cancel."

Billy works to control the Egor part of his mind as he begins his expedition. One quick way to mute that voice when Egor is out of control, is to issue a command to your mind. Repeat the words, "Cancel, Cancel." This is a computer technique that can be employed as a worrying thought arises, that needs to be stopped.

Another method is meditation. Focus your mind for a period of time in silence. The sound of chanting, gentle music or use of a mantra can also help focus your thoughts. A mantra is a word or sound you repeat to yourself, for example, "Om." It's a good idea to choose a mantra that has been suggested by someone with knowledge about meditation methods.

Conversation Points continued...

Edison pressed on for years, maintaining the faith that he would discover the secret to the light bulb, which, he finally did. What a wonderfully strong Adversity Quotient (AQ) he displayed.

Billy must have this same unshakeable faith in his dream, a belief that he will find his new home, despite any challenges he might face. He can do this by choosing his words carefully to be those that reflect an attitude of success. For example, Egor might have encouraged Billy to introduce himself as a lost beaver. Billy decides instead to say, "I am Billy the Beaver and I'm finding a stream to make into a new home." This statement makes it unquestionable that Billy has a clear vision and commitment to achieve his goal. To strengthen this vision, Billy could repeat this affirmation to himself in the morning and at night before he goes to sleep. He could embellish the vision by seeing himself successful and saying out loud, "I am swimming in the cool water of my beautiful new pond." The more detailed you visualize your goal, the more senses you engage, and the more you emotionalize your desire, the more success you will have. If Billy has integrity and always keeps his word, then he can begin to enjoy right now, the great feelings that he will have when he is successful. He has said that he will achieve the goal and it is as good as accomplished. This attitude will be reflected in his confident behaviour. Infinite intelligence will hear and respond to a heartfelt request.

Questions

- How can you strengthen the vision of your goal?

- Are your visions for success pictured as completed goals, or are you trying to establish this ability? The best way to envision your goals is to see yourself living in the final outcome, employing as many senses as you can.

- Uncertainty is one of the most challenging concerns that humanity faces. Think of ways you overcome uncertainty. Test yourself--consider some of the negative news that seems so prevalent. Identify a more positive approach.

Exercises

- Retell this chapter of the story to a supportive person, in your own words. Describe any insights or questions you have.

- Learn about the art of telling stories.

- Edison often congratulated himself on mini-successes that comprised even the things that did not work out. What mini-successes has Billy had?

Write, reflect and discuss...

Knowledge Nugget!

Meditation and Self Care

Knowledge: it is comforting when others believe you can accomplish anything. However, to reach your biggest goals you must start with believing yourself that you can. Learn to love and support yourself, and trust in your abilities.

Possibility Pond

Near the top of the ridge, he saw a dark mound of earth with a small, black hole beneath it. It looked like a bear or a wolf den.

Chapter 7: Advice from Unusual Sources

After Willy wrapped the bug like a sandwich to go, the huge spider turned and looked at Billy with its many eyes. Billy nervously wondered what it was about to do. He wanted to shout, "I'm too big for you to eat!" but before he could, Willy started spinning his web once again.

The spider kept looking at Billy as he worked. It seemed that all Willy wanted was to get on with web building and catch the next meal. While Egor kept Billy busy with worry, Willy was thinking, "This funny looking creature is going to scare all the bugs away; I wonder how I can get him out of my cave?"

Finally, after almost completing the web Willy said, "I've heard there is a stream over the hill." Clinging to the web with five hairy legs, Willy used the other three to point the way. Billy wasn't sure which direction he was pointing and asked Willy to show him again, perhaps using just one leg. Confident that he understood Willy's directions, he assured the spider he'd be on his way first thing in the morning. Willy reluctantly accepted that there would be a guest for one night, and returned to web-building, hurrying to finish, in preparation for catching a nightly collection of delicious bugs for dinner.

Billy was thankful to be able to stay in the cave for the night, although he didn't sleep well. At one point in the night, the distant howl of a coyote woke him from an already fitful sleep. Later, the hooting of an owl overhead startled him. Finally, the frantic flapping of a moth caught in Willy's web woke him for the last time.

At dawn, Billy prepared to leave the safety of the cave and say goodbye to Willy. Not having had much sleep, he decided to check the location of the stream with Willy once more, so he didn't go off in the wrong direction. Willy pointed to the top of a high ridge that lined Happy Valley. Billy set off on the steep climb to where Willy pointed.

Near the top of the ridge, he saw a dark mound of earth with a small, black hole beneath it. It looked like a bear or a wolf den. "Oh no!" said Egor. "Don't go on. You'll get eaten. Go back home, quickly!" Billy looked around frantically and tried his best to ignore Egor. High rocks surrounded each side of the path to the top of the ridge, so the only way to reach it was to go by the den. Billy was afraid, but he knew that he had to remain calm and think quickly. It could be a bad decision to go along with Egor who continued to mutter something about never making it.

Accept Each Other's Differences

Willy and Billy accept each other's differences, such as their appearance and how they communicate. This is a great model for all of us on earth to follow. Although we differ from each other in many ways, accepting those differences creates the opportunity to learn and expand our experience of others and the world, allowing us to become better for it.

LEARNING COMPANION 7

Conversation Points: Observation

The road to any goal or Major Definite Purpose (MDP) has many possible stop signs along the way. Billy has run into another block (adversity), which has triggered Egor to continue attempting to build fear and impossibility in Billy.

If goals were easy to accomplish, many people would be more successful than they are. At this point, Billy demonstrates a number of qualities necessary for the successful completion of an MDP. Keeping his MDP in mind, Billy creates an ability to be open to clues like the one Willy provided. When the spider said, "I've heard that there is a stream over the hill," Billy's mind was free enough from fear and doubt to hear the clue. He also uses a key success principle, Clarify the Communication, when he asks Willy to point to the location of the new stream. There is a saying, "The myth of communication is that it has taken place." You must be sure that it has. Billy clarifies the communication twice just to be sure.

Finally, Billy uses another key success principle, **Keep Moving Forward** (KMF). Moving forward is the only option when new ideas and possibilities emerge. Another way to think of this is to Take Action. By taking action you gain valuable lessons and experience along the way that will ultimately make you stronger. It is easy to change something; it is darn hard to change nothing. Billy doesn't know if the stream over the hill really exists, but he keeps moving forward on his quest with trust and faith in the clues he gets along the way. Even if it turns out that he's going in the wrong direction, he will become stronger for the experience. He will take his mistakes and turn them into a learning that will help him along the way. Notice how important having faith is to the ultimate success of your journey.

Questions

- Did you judge Willy at first? You might have considered him to be of no use in providing helpful ideas for Billy's journey. We are meaning making machines and attempt to put some sort of meaning on everything. Rather than being quick to judge and apply our own meaning, we increase opportunities by being open to possibility.

- What are some ways to suspend judgment?

- What would you do if faced with some of your biggest fears, for example, fear of failure? or fear of uncertainty?

- Go to a mall and try to observe people without judgment (e.g. approx. height & weight, wrinkled t-shirt and dirty blue jeans vs too-tall, too-fat, un-styled, etc.). See how long you can be in a state of non-judgment; make 10 minutes your goal. (You might want to bring your sleeping bag; it could take a while to get up to 10 minutes of non-judgement. ☺) This practice provides an opportunity to change your outlook on life.

Write, reflect and discuss…

_____
_____
_____
_____
_____
_____
_____
_____
_____
_____
_____
_____
_____
_____
_____

Knowledge Nugget!

Observation vs. Judgement

One of the questions asks us to suspend judgment. For example, you might judge someone, "This person is too old," when you first meet them. One way to override judgement is to work on remembering their name by repeating it several times. Another way is to create a visual with their face. For example, when introduced to Barb, you could put a necklace of BARBed wire around her head like a bandanna.

Learning Points: Judgement

To accomplish any goal requires determination and the ability to move beyond challenges. As you proceed toward your goals, think of adversities as working in the same manner as tempering steel to make it stronger. The adversities will make you stronger for your journey as you overcome them. Perhaps you don't currently have skills, attitudes or beliefs that will be necessary for the successful completion of your goal. Perhaps the adversities that seem to block your success will give you something necessary for your journey, when you overcome them. Early American settlers used this philosophy when they selected wood to make wagon wheels. They chose trees that stood alone in fields, trees that had been buffeted by storms and winds yet remained standing when others had broken and fallen. They knew that these lone trees were the strongest because they had withstood the test of time.

They were often ugly and gnarled, and not recognized for their hidden treasure, passed over because of appearance. The early settlers suspended the desire to judge these trees as ugly and inferior, instead appreciating them for their strength. Billy also suspends judgment even though he initially thinks Willy is ugly and scary. By suspending judgment he was able to hear the message Willy had for him.

Always be open to the many ways that a solution may be offered. Often another and better solution is suggested under unusual circumstances. Here, the method a spider uses in the construction of a web may apply to creating a pond and a new home. "How?" you may ask. Read on.

Exercise

- Summarize and retell this chapter of the story in your own words.

- Describe any adversities you have faced and overcome. What were the benefits?

- You will greatly enhance your life by applying these success concepts. Describe what you have begun to use. Notice where your understanding of the principles has created positive change, and where you are living the life you wish to live.

Write, reflect and discuss...

The author in a Vancouver Island coyote den. It was late summer; mother and pups had moved on. I was nervous, but I had my wife with me, and techniques for managing my inner Egor.

Possibility Pond

Am I dreaming, or is that the sound of running water?.

Chapter 8: Pushing Through Adversity

Once Billy calmed his fears and chased Egor away, he looked more closely at the den. He noticed that the earth around it hadn't been disturbed for some time. It was early summer, which meant that the mother and pups had probably abandoned the den in the spring.

"Surely the den will be empty. If there are bears or wolves nearby, they would have smelled me by now," he thought. Billy forced himself to keep moving forward up the hill. He couldn't look into the den as he went by for fear it would draw an animal out to attack him. He was greatly relieved when he finally passed it without detecting any movement from inside. Billy continued the long, steep climb to the top of the hill. Once on top, he flopped on the ground to rest. He had spent days looking for a new stream and had found nothing. He lay there with closed eyes, exhausted. His mouth and huge teeth touched the dry soil. As he lay exhausted, Egor started in again, "What are you doing all alone and so far from home? This whole trip has been a big waste of time." Once again, Billy struggled to calm his mind and concentrate on his vision of a cool stream. As he did this, Egor's negative chatter subsided and he noticed a quiet noise in the distance. He thought, "Am I dreaming or is that the sound of rushing water?" He sat up, and despite his exhaustion, was filled with new energy. Far away in the distance, nestled between two hills, was a fast-flowing stream. Growing along its banks was Billy's favorite food, tender poplar trees. He smacked his lips in anticipation. He hadn't eaten for such a long time and was very thirsty. Billy no longer felt tired, though he wondered how he would keep himself motivated, as the stream would take another day to reach.

LEARNING COMPANION 8

Conversation Points: EndPoint Vision

Once again, Billy proves that he has become the most important member of his **Mastermind Alliance**. His ability to stay positive in the face of Egor's constant doubts and fears is impressive. Yet, attaining major goals often requires more than self-motivation. The assistance of a Mastermind Alliance becomes imperative to the successful completion of complex goals. He must be careful with whom he shares his dream, selecting those willing to support him in positive and practical ways. Dream Suckers are capable of destroying a dream in seconds; Billy will need his wits about him when it comes time to add to his MMA. With only himself in his MMA at this point, Billy needs to muster up as much energy as he can to complete his journey. His goal is in sight but he will require help, both physical and emotional support, to finish his journey.

Having a powerful **EndPoint Visualization** (EPV) of your goal is important to the successful achievement of your MDP. Billy's MDP in 15 words: "There is a stream out there away from humans and I'm going to find it!" needs more detail to keep him full of energy for his journey. He has the start of a great EPV, but he can make the vision of success more tangible by seeing himself in the stream, seeing the pond finished, feeling the emotions of success, and imagining the types of animals that will come to live in his new home. He can see the color of the water, hear the sound of the rushing water and smell the mud that he will use to create the dam. Now is the time for Billy to flesh out his vision of success.

Learning Points: Resilience

"The best do what the rest are not prepared to do."
– Vic Lindal

Billy has been away from home for several days now. Often, when embarking on the pursuit of an MDP, there are certain duties that may be sacrificed. For example, Billy is not caring for his little sister as he had done for the last year. At first, he felt guilty about this, but he realized that he had to move beyond his responsibility as a big brother to fulfill the next phase of his life. By doing so, he may have let Chewie down briefly, however this action creates the important opportunity for Chewie to grow up and fulfill her new role in the family. Those who are unable to get past the initial feeling of guilt at moving on in life and the apparent negative impact that it may have on others, often remain stuck and don't reach their goals.

Write, reflect and discuss…

Knowledge Nugget!

Do the Matador Walk When You Are Tired, Nervous or Need to Inspire Yourself

Billy is very tired and he could begin to wonder if he would even have the energy to return home. This is where he must Go the Extra Mile (GEM). Successful people do what others may be reluctant to do. Billy will learn Success Principles as his story unfolds. Here are others that apply: Faith, A Positive Attitude, Enthusiasm, Self-discipline, Teamwork, Determination, and Take Action.

Remember to be a participant in the story. Engage your senses and your imagination to connect to the story. Pretend you're Billy and need to reset your mind and your negative Egor. When you are feeling nervous or down, take a deep breath, stand up, smile and step forward. Did you feel the positive effect? Matadors do this during bull fights. Also goalies in sports can become negative when scored upon, and then do not perform well. This is a useful action to take as you are about to do a presentation. The Matador Walk will reenergize and focus you.

Questions

- Are your goals well defined with details of how they would look, feel, smell, taste and sound when you have achieved them? Y/N?

- Have you drawn a picture of your EPV and also written it out on paper? Y/N?

- Have you ever had to muster up the courage to reach one of your goals--similar to that required for walking by a bear den? Y/N

- Have you ever experienced exhaustion on the path to your goal, only to be revived by a new development or vision? Y/N? This happens when you Keep Moving Forward (KMF), for example: your MMA introduces new ideas.

- Have you ever felt guilty leaving some role or responsibility behind to grow into the next phase of your life and/or job? Y/N?

- Who would you have in your Mastermind Alliance? List the people and share the list with someone else. **You cannot successfully complete a journey without taking others with you.**

- What have you sacrificed in reaching for a goal?

- In your opinion, how is Billy shutting down Egor's negative chatter?

Exercises

- Retell this chapter of the story in your own words. How is Billy doing, shutting down Egor's negative chatter?

- Be a participant in the story. Engage your senses and imagination to connect to the story. Pretend you are Billy and need to reset your mind to respond to the negativity of Egor.

- Sit down, take a deep breath and then stand up and smile. Did you feel the positive effect? Step forward strongly, do your Matador Walk.

- Consider this statement: You walk into the picture you imagine of your future. If it is a positive one (Possibility Pond), or a negative one (Impossible Creek), which do you think will prevail?

- Think of different phases of Billy's journey so far. There is a popular quote, "it's not the destination, but the journey." List what you consider to be the positive stages in Billy's Journey, and the negative ones.

Write, reflect and discuss…

_____
_____
_____
_____
_____
_____
_____
_____
_____
_____
_____
_____
_____
_____
_____
_____
_____
_____
_____
_____

Knowledge Nuggets!

"Life is not measured by the number of breaths, but by the moments that take your breath away."

If you were Billy, would your breath have been taken away by the vision of a possible home, or by seeing a coyote that you had to walk by? Why, or why not?

Believe in Your Success

You can only think a thought if you have the words and language for it. Choose your words carefully. If you repeatedly say a challenge is impossible, you will believe it is impossible, and that will be the likely outcome. Notice the language you use. **You will be right, whether you think you can or you think you can't.** Believe in success. A positive belief is a critical asset.

As he was telling his story to his colony, he could see some beavers smirking.

Chapter 9: Guarding Your Vision

Billy began to daydream about damming the steam to form his own pond. "I'll build my own lodge after the water fills in behind the dam," he thought. He could clearly imagine his new home built of poplar branches and mud packed tightly together.

He could also envision all the animals coming to live in and around his pond. The squawking of ducks and the giant nest of the blue heron were clear in his mind's eye. Billy could hear the geese swirling overhead and smell the pine tree scent wafting through his nostrils. As he emerged from his daydream, he knew that he would achieve his goal. "I'm going to go home and tell everyone I've found the best stream in the world," he said to himself. It was easy for Billy to return to Happy Valley; the trip did not seem so difficult going back. As he walked on his journey, Billy nibbled the bottoms of trees. By doing this he could easily follow the markers back to the stream.

Billy reached his parents' house on the water near daybreak. His family and other beavers had spent the night before, as they often did, fixing the latest hole Farmer Ed had blasted in their dam. Billy heard them say, "We'll outsmart Farmer Ed someday." He swam toward them quickly; he could hardly keep himself from shouting as he told the other beavers about his discovery.

He told them about his vision of the stream with the animals and all the tasty poplar trees, all without any humans in sight. But, as he was telling his story, he could see the other beavers smirking. He found this puzzling. Finally, as he finished his story, the other beavers burst out laughing and one said, "That's Impossible Creek. It's too strong to dam up, Billy; you'll never stop it." All the other beavers laughed and looked at Billy as if he had lost his mind. They went back to fixing the damage Farmer Ed had done the day before.

Possibility Pond

LEARNING COMPANION 9

Conversation Points: Resistance

Billy is excited about the stream he found and he wants to return home to share the details of his dream with his family and friends. At this point, Billy needs the support of a Mastermind Alliance, surrounding himself with individuals who can see and focus on all the reasons why his dream can work, not on why it can't. Yet, he isn't careful with whom he shares his dream and his ideas get shot down as a result. The beavers he thought would be excited for him, ridiculed his ideas instead. Even many of his family members don't seem to support him. For the moment, he is demoralized and depressed instead of supported and energized.

Billy has gained valuable experience in his battles with Egor, and this will serve him well when he is faced with another adversity.

Learning Points: Allies

During any quest to reach a goal, we often find ourselves needing support from an ally. At times like this it is critical to choose people who can see the possibilities. "Go to Solution and Not Problem!" should be the rallying cry.

Unfortunately, your own family can often be the worst candidates for your MMA. Their love for you can act as a barrier to your success as they often don't want you to take risks. Or, like the flies on the windowsill, they may be stuck in a repetitive pattern of behavior they don't realize can be improved upon. My father told me an interesting story about what he called Crabology. A fisherman on a beach was using crabs for bait and kept them in a can with low sides. Any one crab could have easily climbed out of the can, but none ever did. He asked the fisherman why. The fisherman reported that when one crab crawls up the side, the others invariably drag him back into the can.

Questions

- Who is part of your Mastermind Alliance?
- Who in your family is not part of your MMA?
- Who in your family would you choose to support your goals and why?
- Have you ever shared your vision with someone, only to be shut down with reasons why you can't succeed? How did that feel?
- Something is only as bad as your reaction to it. Is Billy in a bad situation?

There is a Reason for Everything.

Take a moment to let this idea sink in. Billy's reaction to disappointment and setback allows him to contemplate a huge mindset lesson: It is a higher level thought, worth discussing with others. Once Billy comes to trust the idea, he can be comforted by the phrase *without knowing the reason itself*.

This statement requires you to think and to ponder deeply to get your mind around the idea and finally to understand it and then use it. This idea allows you to *relax*. When you are no longer trying to figure out why something has happened and have moved on, the stress is removed and your mind functions much more effectively.

Write, reflect and discuss…

_____
_____
_____
_____
_____
_____
_____
_____
_____
_____
_____
_____

To do something, you need to imagine it first.

You can't enter into new territory physically or intellectually if you don't first imagine it into existence. The ability to dream and go beyond what seems impossible is important to enable you to move toward success and to enjoy the journey.

You can see Crabology in action when Billy returns home. Most of the other beavers are so stuck in their 'can' that they can't support Billy in his efforts, and can't crawl out to something new.

Jeff Bezos, founder of Amazon, is now one of the richest people in the world, but at one time he was told by a knowledgeable person that his Amazon business idea was not worthy.

A strategy for greatly increasing your chances for success is to **Go the Extra Mile**. Apply yourself fully in everything you do, and frequently do those things that are beyond the call of duty. Helping people solve their problems, can lead you to a solution for your own.

The best do what the rest are not prepared to do.

Exercises

- Retell this chapter of the story in your own words.

- Your subconscious mind can be a great ally in achieving your goals. It can constantly work on them even when you are asleep. Think of some of the ways that you can plant ideas in your subconscious so that it can work on your MDP.

- Describe a time where you have experienced adversity and how you overcame it. For me, adversity started with a medical diagnosis and a heart problem. I was told to do no physical labour. I still needed to breathe so I took a breathing course led by people from India. After two months of no physical exercise but a consistent breath practice, I could play hockey without being out of breath. This resulted in me going to India for yoga training.

Choose how Adversity Affects You

The beaver that Billy is today has been shaped by many life experiences. Having many in his colony, including his parents, initially be against his efforts and not supporting his dream was a challenge for Billy. How he chooses to react to this adversity impacts his success in life. When faced with adversity many people react poorly and then continue to tell the story of how bad the adversity was … playing the "Ain't it awful," game in discussions with others. They choose to let the adversity define them as a victim rather than using it as an opportunity to learn, and as a stepping stone to becoming a better person.

Write, reflect and discuss…

_____
_____
_____
_____
_____
_____
_____
_____
_____
_____
_____
_____
_____
_____
_____
_____

My Personal Health Journey

For me, one adversity began with a medical diagnosis and a potential heart problem. I was told by a doctor to not do any physical labour until a heart specialist saw me. I still needed to breathe, so I took a course on breathing, which my wife found, given by an instructor from India. After two months of doing no physical exercise, but plenty of breath work, I was amazed that I could play hockey without being winded. Learning to breathe and exercise my lungs from these knowledgeable people led to me going to India and learning to be a yoga instructor. It was a fabulous experience. The end result was dramatic. Can you think of an example in your life that illustrates the idea that "behind every adversity is the seed of an equal or greater opportunity, if you but look"? When faced with adversity, we are forced to **consider** other options, and they are often superior choices, at least in my experience. Learning powerful, alternative ways of breathing has led me to a healthier life. I have never been disappointed by the unexpected.

Possibility Pond

If everyone thinks your dream is foolish then surely it must not be possible.

Chapter 10: Finding Allies

Later that night, while lying in bed, Billy felt sadder than he had ever been in his life. In the dark of their bedroom, he shared with his little sister what had happened. Chewie shivered and squealed with fear when Billy described Willy the spider with his eight hairy legs and many eyes.

He kicked his paws up on the bottom of Chewie's top bunk as he told her about the bear or coyote den he had come upon, making her jump with fear. When listening to Billy's story Chewie rolled, bounced and laughed from her top bunk. Billy's mother heard the noise and came in to tell them to be quiet and get to sleep. As she left the room she said, "Billy, why can't you be like all the rest of the beavers and find a slow-moving steam on flat land nearby. That way it will be easy to build your dam." After saying goodnight to their mother, Billy sunk down in his bunk in despair. He was losing hope in the face of everyone's opinions.

Egor started in, "If everyone thinks your dream is foolish then surely it must not be possible. How could a little beaver like you stop Impossible Creek?" Just when it seemed like he was losing his battle with Egor's fears and doubts, Chewie leaned over her bunk and looked at Billy. In a serious voice she said, "I believe in your dream Billy. It's a great thing to do." Chewie's support was just what Billy needed to get control of his thoughts again. He had an idea and asked, "Will you come with me Chewie?" She responded with an enthusiastic, "YES!" He didn't know how a young beaver could help, but he knew that he needed her support.

LEARNING COMPANION 10

Conversation Points: Criticism

When Billy's mother leaves, he feels dejected. At first, **he takes all the criticism and teasing from others personally and starts to doubt his own vision**. Yet, with his playful sister, he finds the energy to tell his story one more time, even jazzing it up to get her to laugh. It ends up that Billy has a believer in Chewie. She tells him what a great idea she thinks he has, which is just the support he needs at this critical time. This support is one of the roles of a Mastermind Alliance.

He asks his sister if she would join him on his journey, and she says yes. Finally, Billy has another member in his MMA other than himself. Support of this kind, even if it is from one person, is critical at times when serious doubts and challenging circumstances set in. An MMA can start off small, but once events begin to happen, other people will see the passion you have for your dream and join in to support the idea. Choose additional members of your MMA carefully and with the support of current members. Working together without discord is most important.

Learning Points: Perspective

An important point to remember while pursuing your dream is **Don't Take Criticism Personally**. It has been suggested that at least 95% of what people say when reacting to us is actually a reaction that they are having to a previous event in *their* lives. So, when people react to us, they are most likely reacting to something totally unrelated to us. This supports the idea of not taking criticism personally, as in most cases of criticism, it's not about you. The importance of carefully selecting members of your Mastermind Alliance becomes clearer at this point in Billy's journey. Seeking out individuals who believe in your dream when the going gets rough becomes critical during times of doubt and setbacks.

Billy could spend time and energy wondering why the other beavers reacted so negatively about his quest, especially his mother, who from her perspective had Billy's best interest in mind. This would take his attention away from his MDP. One of the most important spiritual truths to remember at times like this is: Everything Is as It Should Be. When you accept what has taken place in this way, instead of focusing on what might have been or who's at fault, you are prepared to look for positive options instead of getting stuck. Worrying, trying to place blame, or feeling badly means you are focused on something other than your MDP. Your brain does not work effectively under these circumstances and it becomes harder to find solutions to the inevitable blocks that come up.

A true entrepreneur knows that opportunities may initially appear as adversities. Criticism is just another adversity. Instead of feeling badly, Billy could be considering alternative possibilities or, watching for opportunities that will assist him in achieving his dream. He is the key to the success of his dream and he must continue to believe in his goal even if the situation does not look good.

Write, reflect and discuss...

_____
_____
_____
_____
_____
_____
_____
_____
_____

Knowledge Nuggets!

You cannot be successful unless you take others with you.

Others can help you form a Mastermind Alliance. Ideas for Billy selecting the members are critical, and is covered in a leader section of this book. A Mastermind Alliance involves two or more people who work in perfect Harmony for the attainment of a definite purpose. Through the Mastermind Alliance you may borrow and use the education, experience, influence and financial support of other people.

The Blueberry Pie Syndrome:

Kindness and selflessness builds others up. When my youngest son Rob was very small, he observed his brothers and Dad lamenting that there was no more blueberry pie, because they had devoured it. He still had his piece, and I heard his small voice pipe up and say, "You can have my piece." This selfless act has not only stuck with me all these years, but it reminds me to be a better person.

I grew from this experience, and we can all find ways to help others grow to be their best.

Possibility Pond

Keeping his focus on the dream will help him shed the criticism. He must be The Keeper of the Faith. Believe in his goal, gather others for his MMA and Keep Moving Forward. Also, Billy could practice an attitude of gratitude and be thankful for where he is now, having completed a remarkable and exciting journey that has tremendous promise. He has started to grow in his ability as an adventurous beaver.

When Billy chooses Chewie to help, he is beginning to form an MMA. What does Chewie bring to the MMA at the stage? I believe the positive influence she brings is significant at this stage of Billy's goal. Watch who is added to Billy's MMA. Who in the story would you choose?

Questions
- How would you have felt if you were Billy and you were laughed at?
- How would you react to that type of criticism?
- What opportunities are available to Billy at this time?
- Have you ever taken someone's criticism personally?
- Have you ever criticized someone for a reason that didn't have anything to do with them?

Exercise
- Retell this chapter of the story in your own words.

80% of Business Partnerships Fall Apart

That is double the divorce rate!. It is likely that failed partnerships were not constructed with the ideas of a Mastermind Alliance (MMA). To inoculate a relationship from break-up (business or personal), it is critical to internalize the rules for an MMA given here and in later sections of the story. My wife and I are well versed in MMA and keep it at the fore front of our minds to keep our relationship healthy, happy and always growing.

Time is your life currency

Whenever you are making a decision, a useful question to keep in mind is "If time is my life currency (it has value), how do I choose to spend it?" This implies that you need to spend it wisely. Billy set off on a perilous journey before gathering support which would have taken time. Billy possesses an unconscious rule to "never waste a minute."

Time seemed more precious when the beavers' lives were threatened by farmer Ed's active threats. Because of constant threats, not only from Farmer Ed, but also from predators such as bears, Billy was keenly aware his life was defined by the space between his birth and death. He began to realize that what he chooses to do within that space (his life) must be of great value to him. You might find the idea of dying to be dreadful or frightening, however, the country of Bhutan is listed as one of the happiest countries in the world, and the citizens contemplate death five times a day. Would you consider your death even once a day for 5 minutes to cultivate your happiness and sense of gratitude?

Write, reflect and discuss...

_____
_____
_____
_____
_____
_____
_____
_____
_____
_____
_____
_____
_____
_____

Chewie jumped into the stream and slapped her tail. Billy thought there was real danger.

The next time someone hurts or disappoints you, let them.

That thought may surprise you. Here is the opportunity: Rather than wasting your valuable energy on things that you could never have controlled in the first place, move on and maintain your happiness.

Possibility Pond

Chapter 11: Asking at the Risk of Receiving

Billy spent the night alternating between doubt and belief in his dream. The next morning he asked Chewie again if she'd help him dam Impossible Creek. To his surprise, she offered an enthusiastic, "Yes!" Before anyone was awake, Billy and Chewie set off to Impossible Creek.

By following the marked trail, and with the extra energy their partnership provided, they reached the top of Happy Valley quickly.

Although Chewie was smaller than Billy, she easily kept up to him because she was so excited. Soon they were beside Impossible Creek. The water rushed by making such a loud roaring noise that it almost drowned out the soft sound of the wind moving through the trees. "Ahhhh, the air is so fresh and clean," said Billy. "Look Chewie, there are beautiful flowers everywhere!" As he scanned the valley, Billy saw their favorite food everywhere, young poplar trees!

They felt as though they were in a candy shop. Billy began to relax. He said, "Chewie, if you see danger, slap your tail on the water as a warning, and then dive into the creek where you will be safe."

Billy and Chewie snacked on the tender poplar shoots before they began their work on the dam. They were excited and full of energy as they worked to make Billy's vision a reality. They began cutting down poplar trees to make a great dam.

They worked all day long without stopping. Chewie could see Billy's dream. Throughout the day they shared visions of how the stream would look when it was dammed. Billy's dream had become Chewie's dream too.

They were happy about building a new home and had fun, often laughing for no particular reason. Once Chewie even jumped into the stream and slapped her tail on the water to scare Billy into thinking there was danger. Billy scrambled quickly and dove into the creek.

Chewie thought this was a great joke and laughed heartily. Billy cautioned her saying, "Don't do that again Chewie. There is real danger around us and I don't want to think you are fooling me when real danger comes along." Chewie promised only to slap her tail if there was real and present danger.

When evening arrived, they had cut down enough poplar trees to start building the dam. Together, using their strong teeth, they dragged the large trees to the creek. As the tree trunks touched the rushing water, they were swept downstream by the current and out of sight. Billy and Chewie tried time and time again to get the trees to block the river, but log after log disappeared down Impossible Creek.

LEARNING COMPANION 11

Conversation Points: Doubt

Ask at The Risk of Receiving is a powerful habit that rewards those who use it.

Despite the many doubtful voices and thoughts presented to Billy by Egor during the night, he asks Chewie to help him dam Impossible Creek. Again she says, "Yes." If Billy had not asked her for help, Chewie would not have known he needed assistance. Once asked, she could decide if she was willing to support Billy's dream by helping dam the creek. Others can't read our minds and may not be aware of what we need. By Asking at the Risk of Receiving we give those around us the opportunity to make a choice and assist us, or not. In this way we begin to establish clear communication with our MMA.

Another success principle that is illustrated as Billy and Chewie work to dam the creek is the opportunity to learn when presented with adversity. The trees they have taken all day to cut down are not big enough to block Impossible Creek and they are now faced with another need to creatively problem solve. Life lessons can show up looking like adversities or frustrations. I have a friend who lacks integrity, in that he doesn't keep his word. He says he'll do something and then doesn't follow through. He often complains that he has people working for him that have this same trait. Life lessons have a habit of using the people in our lives to mirror our own lesson to us. My friend may always find himself surrounded by unreliable people if he doesn't pay attention to the lessons delivered from the universe. If Billy doesn't learn to believe in himself, other beavers that don't believe in themselves would most likely surround him.

Questions

- Do you ask for help? Are you concerned about the possibility of rejection?
- What could you ask someone to help you do that you currently don't believe they would say yes to?
- Look up the meaning of 'integrity'.
- Do you have integrity (strong moral principles)? Do you keep your word? Always?
- List the people in your life who have integrity.
- Do you have a problem that keeps showing up in other people? What does that mean when selecting members of your MMA?

- Practice the No exercise. Ask people for help when you know the answer is, "No." Notice what happens.

This is an opportunity to explore new ideas at an important juncture in the story. Can you think of anything that Billy and Chewie might try to solve the challenge that they find themselves in? You might try brainstorming or Mind Mapping--the premier method for idea generation--to green light for new ideas.

Question	Response

Knowledge Nugget!

"Laughter is a way to shorten the road."
– Irish saying

Billy cautions Chewie to not slap her tail on the water when there is no danger. When you are on a journey with others, the idea of not fooling around can be front and centre.

Humourist, Doug Larson tells us, "The ageing process has us firmly in its grip if you never get the urge to throw a snowball." He is telling us there is a time for humour, and that humour is important to a team on a journey. However it shouldn't have a negative impact.

Learning Points: Risk Asking

I am the Co-Founder of We Care Home Health Care Services. Our head office was located in a small, Manitoba town, and the company needed a more central location for a Canada-wide presence and for company meetings. We had the idea of calling George Cohon, the head of the Canadian McDonalds, and asking for help. At first, it seemed like an unrealistic request to make. However, Mr. Cohen responded in a magnanimous way, immediately appointing one of his executives to the We Care board and opening their Toronto corporate office for We Care board meetings at no charge. **Powerful actions and success come from "Ask at the Risk of Receiving".**

Sometimes we sabotage our efforts to find help with our own doubts that people will come to our aid. A short story will illustrate this point. A man was going to ask his neighbor for the use of his wheelbarrow. As he walked over to the neighbour's home he began to think, "I bet he'll tell me that he's using the wheel barrow." A few steps later he thought, "I bet he'll tell me that he already lent the wheelbarrow to another neighbor." During the last few steps to the neighbour's door he thinks, "I bet he doesn't even want to lend me the wheel barrow." As he knocks on the neighbour's door, these internal doubts, his own Egor, finally get the best of him. When the neighbor opens the door he says, "Keep your stupid wheelbarrow then." This humorous short story illustrates the importance of keeping Egor in check and focusing on the positives and possibilities.

Taking action is always important. A Mantra[1] to keep in mind is: "I can always change something; it is darn hard to change nothing."

Exercises

- Retell this chapter of the story in your own words.

- Share the story with someone who can offer constructive feedback and new ideas.

---

[1] Mantra: a sound, word, slogan or statement that is repeated to aid concentration and internalize an idea.

Write, reflect and discuss...

Knowledge Nugget!

Finding the Joy, Making it Joyful

I had the luxury of learning to build my own cottage with a man who became my mentor, French Canadian carpenter Mr. Martin Marion. It seemed as though he was never worn down, regardless of how long we worked in a day. His amusement showed up in wrinkles as he smiled and took the time to find things to laugh about. It was a joy to work with him. Some of the building process was daunting, rough terrain, high roofs, etc. However, he approached each task as though it were a bit of fun, and so the path was always shortened.

I wasn't sure we could accomplish some of the features in the build, but with him, we would start toward a destination I eventually found we could reach. Working on this book with Sandy and Dan always brought enjoyment. Starting a journey needs to have a pause at the start where these ideas are made clear to all. A positive mental attitude is important, but also, identifying how it will show up is essential.

They were a long way from the safety of their Happy Valley home.

Chapter 12: There Has to be a Way

Chewie couldn't stand to see their hard work float away. She hung onto one small tree like a tenacious bulldog. The fast-flowing waters sucked her in and dragged her downstream. When she realized she could no longer see Billy, Chewie finally let go.

Billy thought he might have to jump in and save her, but Chewie made it to the shore on her own.

He laughed when he saw how determined Chewie was, and he was relieved that she was safe. At the end of the day, they were both exhausted. "Maybe we can't do it Billy," whispered Chewie in a questioning voice. But Billy didn't answer. At this moment he couldn't imagine how to place a log so it wouldn't float away and would hold added logs to make a dam. There had to be a way. Then Egor chimed in, "The other beavers are right, why do you think they call it Impossible Creek?"

Exhausted, Billy stopped Egor and quietly said to Chewie "Let's go home." As they started the long trek home, Billy was thinking about their failure to dam the creek, and he dreaded being laughed at. They felt more tired than they should be for such a journey.

Moving slower than they had on their way to Impossible Creek made their return journey more dangerous for Chewie. Predators would attack her first since she was smaller than Billy. She would be an easy meal for owls and bobcats. She'd be but a snack for a bear. They walked for a long time, stopping often to listen to the sounds in the forest for signs of danger. They were a long way from the safety of their Happy Valley home.

As they came around one corner, in the shadows they heard an eerie noise. It was a whimpering, beaver-like sound. Chewie looked at Billy to see if he heard what she did. "Someone is hurt." Billy whispered. "It sounds like another beaver," said Chewie in a trembling voice. Billy nodded in agreement and wondered what another beaver would be doing far from water and in such a dangerous area. "Run, Billy." whispered Chewie in a soft voice, and then she turned and started quickly down the trail.

Possibility Pond

LEARNING COMPANION 12

Conversation Points: Failure

Chewie and Billy attempt to dam Impossible Creek and they are not successful. Let's reframe this obstacle. All this failure demonstrates is that **two young beavers, with limited knowledge were not able to dam the stream yet**. It doesn't prove that it can't be done. This is a great example of **reframing a challenge**, a useful problem solving tool.

At this point in the story, one solution to this challenge would be for Billy to increase the size of his Mastermind Alliance. By doing so, he increases the chances that he will get the expertise he needs for his goal. During any quest for a goal, the challenge is to convince others of the viability of your dream. As before, Billy must remain positive in the face of his sister's doubt. Billy must continue to have faith and keep his vision clear. The whimpering sound scares Chewie because she immediately judges it as a sign of danger. But, as with Willy the spider, Billy is tuned into clues from his environment and he listens to the sound for a while before making a decision.

Learning Points: Growth

One of life's greatest lessons is to **learn to overcome failure. A good start is to reframe, replacing the limiting word** *failure* **with the word** *adversity*. When you are in life's training ground or in a necessary preparation, then you will be strengthened by these challenging experiences rather than weakened. We often learn the most from our failures. Some philosophers believe that a life without adversity is truly an impoverished one. When you press on in the face of adversity, your personal growth will lead you to success. Many parents do everything to help their children avoid failure. **Failure is an opportunity to grow, and when we teach our children the value of failure, we truly do our children a service.** The story of the silk worm, illustrates this point. If you assist a silk worm as it struggles to get out of the cocoon, it will die. It needs the struggle to fully develop.

Questions

- How would you dam the creek? Think of as many ideas as you can without judging them as being good or bad, viable or impossible. For example, in 5 minutes, three teenage girls thought of 24 options for damming the creek.

- What words do you use for failure?

- What mental software do you run about yourself and your goals? Are your words positive or self-defeating? Can you control your thoughts?

- Have you ever tried to stop a negative thought? Billy learned to say the words, "Cancel, Cancel", or "Delete, Delete". What do you do when negative thoughts come up that are not useful?

This practice can be helpful with a variety of experiences. For example, during those times when you are trying to get to sleep and thoughts keep rising in your mind. If you replace the words Cancel, Cancel or Delete, Delete with the sound of Om, it can be repeated as a mantra and become a method for meditating.

Meditation is Mind Training

Meditation is a marvelous method for training your mind to do what you wish it to do. It is a practice that involves focusing your mind using a combination of mental and physical techniques. Depending on the type of meditation you choose, you can meditate to relax, reduce anxiety and stress, or go into the silence. Many say you can stop the dancing monkeys (thoughts in the mind) by meditating, which will allow you to focus when you want to.

The Celtic people of Ireland, used the following form of meditation, especially when trying to sleep. You first remember the happiest day of your life, and recreate it again in your mind. Then learn to go into that same feeling of happiness with as much detail as you can. This would certainly help Billy get to sleep in the challenging location he has chosen. It is something that you would benefit from trying.

Notice Synchronicities

Synchronicity is the experience of two apparently related things happening close together in time, with no discernable direct cause. The same day I wrote about this useful technique for dispelling negative thoughts, my son Jon in Calgary, 3,180 kilometers away, called. During our conversation, he mentioned his day had been tough, and he had used this technique, which I had taught him many years ago. He said that it had made such a positive difference to his day. I recommend that you practice this technique to help you reduce negative thoughts and improve your ability to experience positive options. Also, keep track of your synchronicities; they can be inspiring. When we value them, they seem to appear more often.

Learning Points continued...

The words you use along the way to your goal are crucial. As the difference between failure and adversity demonstrate, words have a powerful impact on the way we think and feel. They are important elements of any affirmation, and our daily conversations and thoughts must be watched for defeating words, and then to change them. Egor knows this. He reminds Billy that Impossible Creek didn't get its name by accident. Without realizing it, every time Billy talks about the creek and uses its name, he reinforces the idea that it is impossible to dam. Our subconscious mind is like a powerful computer that runs on software defined by our words and thoughts. Choosing the software we run our brain with requires carefully worded positive affirmations and thoughts. What we say to ourselves and to others tends to define our actions and our reality. Surround yourself with positive people. When you listen to negative opinions, either directly or indirectly, this gives the opinions power, and you begin to think in this way yourself. The result is you will be much less likely to have a positive outcome.

Inside their heads and hearts, the challenge to dam the creek seems to be beyond their ability. It does not matter how far out of reach, or whether it seems impossible, what Billy and Chewie will learn is that alone and together their limits lie much further out than they can imagine. They will learn a valuable lesson: there is no such thing as a hopeless situation.

By placing tree trunks in the water and observing what happens, this positive action will lead to questions and understandings of the bigger goal, and possible solutions to achieve the bigger goal of constructing a pond that supports a colony of beavers.

Exercise
- Retell this chapter of the story in your own words.

Write, reflect and discuss…

___

Knowledge Nugget!

Determination = Commitment to Success

It is important to understand the definition of words. We cannot think a thought, unless we have the language. Billy and Chewie must be determined in their adventure. Here is a definition for the success principal, Determination: the commitment to take action and achieve your goals despite the challenges you may experience. People who express determination continue to work to achieve their goals, regardless of other factors. Another definition is the ability to continue trying to do something, even if it is difficult. I was proud of my son Jon's determination when he won the Digger Award in two hockey tournaments.

Billy frantically looked for a way to open the cage. Nothing seemed to work ... yet.

Chapter 13: Going the Extra Mile

Billy turned to follow Chewie, but stopped and said, "I need to see who's in trouble, Chewie." Billy didn't know why he was going back; all he knew was that someone needed help. Billy moved quietly toward the moaning sound. Chewie was silent as she followed her brother.

Billy gently slapped his tail on the ground to warn her to stop. Coming closer to the edge of a clearing, he saw a large beaver trapped in a cage. To the left, Billy could hear the sound of human voices as they sat talking around a crackling fire. He instinctively knew that the humans were bear hunters and the old beaver in the cage was to be used as bait. The hunters knew that bears love to eat beavers more than anything. They planned to lure bears with the bait, and then shoot them.

Billy flicked his leathery tail slightly to signal Chewie to be quiet and to stay where she was. Billy began crawling slowly toward the cage. He felt braver knowing that Chewie was there watching out for him. A harsh laugh from the hunters rang out in the forest and Billy jumped. "Did they hear me?" he asked Chewie quietly, "I don't want us to be bear bait." He listened carefully and sighed with relief when he didn't hear anyone coming. Billy continued to crawl toward the cage and once it was in view he could clearly see that a weak, elderly beaver was imprisoned. The beaver saw Billy, but he was too weak to speak. Guiding his paws around the cage, Billy frantically looked for a way to open it. Nothing seemed to work ... yet.

He could hear the hunters finishing their dinner. He was afraid they would come to the cage when they were done and find him. He had never seen a cage before and he didn't know how to open it. He wiggled anything that he could touch. Finally, one piece moved and Billy could lift the door open a crack. The elderly beaver could sense freedom and pushed on the door with his nose. As Elder crawled out, the steel door clanged shut making a loud sound, vibrating like a bell. One of the hunters yelled, "What was that?" and started running toward the cage.

LEARNING COMPANION 13

Conversation Points: Being Called

Billy is on his journey to find a new home, yet he willingly risks his life and that of his sister to help someone in danger. This type of action demonstrates a success principle called **Going the Extra Mile**. Billy's selfless act of kindness will start a natural process by which his efforts will be repaid in double or triple. There is a law in nature that works like this: **When you give more than expected and you do so without the expectation of return, sooner or later your efforts will be repaid.** In fact, every major and enduring achievement is based on this principle of Going the Extra Mile. Often, in any journey, it is these pivotal acts of giving that ensure your success.

In the art of Going the Extra Mile, intelligence must be considered. Be smart about where you place your efforts. The saying, "Don't plant seeds in rocky ground", is an example of this. Again, Billy faces adversity and meets it with action, instead of fear. He continues to keep his mind positive and doesn't focus on the negatives in his experience.

The successful individual, who lives their Major Definite Purpose, must also consider what they will give back to the world. They must consider contributing in some way as they travel on their path to personal success. When Billy puts aside his fear to help Elder, he is choosing to contribute to the well-being of another, even at the risk of being side tracked from his goal or worse, being harmed. When clarifying one's Major Definite Purpose, the plan must include the kind of contribution you will make to the world in gratitude.

Questions

- Have you ever gone the extra mile? Make a list of these times.
- Have you ever done a selfless act of kindness? What could you do today to Go the Extra Mile toward a goal you have, or to make a difference in someone's life?
- Have you ever helped someone, only to find that they end up helping you more in the long run?
- By helping them, did you get ideas that benefited yourself? The universe is generous.
- Would you have stopped to free Elder, given how dangerous an act it would be? Why?

Write, reflect and discuss…

Knowledge Nugget!

Be Willing to Act on Intuition and Faith.

Earlier we suggested you live on the risk curve and intentionally take risks, so that you do not come to the end of your life wishing you had done more. Billy has to decide if he will try to rescue Elder at this time, given the danger posed by the hunters. It turns out later that Elder is a key factor leading to Billy's success. Perhaps the words intuition and faith are helpful in this discussion.

Possibility Pond

Learning Points: Going Beyond

The mind often finds it easier to focus on all the things that can go wrong instead of on positive outcomes. Try the following: Think of something you did recently and make a list of the things you liked about it and a list of the things that you could improve upon. If you are like most people, you likely found the list of criticisms easier to make and longer than the list of things that you did that you liked. It is important to train your mind to look for the positive. **Going the Extra Mile can help you to build positive thinking.** Make it part of your daily experience and build this positive habit. **One way to do this is by practising random acts of kindness.** Open the door for someone elderly, or offer to carry their groceries. Or, give everyone you meet a small gift. It could be in the form of a kind thought, a compliment, a wild flower or just a smile. By Going the Extra Mile, you will find that life experiences become more positive and opportunities will increase. When you teach your children to Go the Extra Mile, their character will benefit and the habit will serve them well throughout their lives.

Another way to **Go the Extra Mile is to give your services, at no cost, to causes you are interested in.** This is particularly helpful when you are looking for a job. A famous story illustrates this point: Mr. Barnes knew this concept when he volunteered to be the famous Edison's clean-up boy just to be around the inventor.

His Major Definite Purpose was to be Edison's partner, but he had to show his selfless dedication to Edison for two years before he was finally given an opportunity to demonstrate his business skills. Edison gave Barnes a chance to sell the Dictaphone, an invention no one else believed in. Barnes successfully sold this invention and went on to be Edison's partner. This was his original goal and he was willing to Go the Extra Mile to get there.

A wonderful example of Going the Extra Mile occurs when you hear a compliment about someone, and you take the time to pass the compliment on to that person. There are many ways to keep Go the Extra Mile top of mind.

Exercise
- Retell this chapter of the story in your own words.

Write, reflect and discuss…

Grabbing his gun, he ran toward them, and fired. The bullet crashed into a tree next to the beavers.

Possibility Pond

Chapter 14: Finding Allies in Unusual Places

Billy and Chewie scrambled away with Elder as fast as they could. The hunter ran up to the cage and then called to the other hunters for help. He swung around and spotted Billy, Chewie and Elder near the edge of the clearing. Grabbing his gun, he ran toward them, and fired.

The bullet crashed into a tree next to the beavers. The hunter knew the beaver was excellent bait, dead or alive. The cannon-like sound in the quiet forest made the beavers jump with fear and they ran even faster. Luckily it was dusk and the beaver's dark fur coats blended in with the forest.

Billy was thankful that he and Chewie had taken the time to clean their fur before setting off, a task they really didn't want to do because they were so tired. But, if they hadn't cleaned themselves they would be covered with light coloured wood chips and dust that would make them easier to be seen in the shadows, and would possibly leave a trail for the hunters to follow.

The beavers scrambled down a steep slope and hid, barely breathing, being as quiet as possible. In seconds, Billy could hear all the hunters searching around the forest, frantically looking for them. One of the hunters began to walk slowly toward their hiding place as though he knew where they were. Billy wondered if he had seen them. They were in a panic! Should they bolt and run for it? If they did, surely they would be shot. They sat quietly, not even blinking, with their whiskers trembling.

The hunter was so close they thought he would step on them. At that moment, another hunter called and he stopped. He appeared to look right at the beavers, and then he turned and headed back toward the others. They were safe for the moment. Billy, Chewie and Elder didn't move.

After looking everywhere for the beavers, the hunters gave up their search. The beavers waited in the dark forest for what seemed to be forever, just in case they would be heard. Finally, they began moving quietly toward home.

Elder's muscles were tired and sore from his long stay in the cage. As he began to recover, Billy and Chewie asked him how he was trapped.

Elder answered thoughtfully, "It seems so long ago that I set out to find a new home. Farmer Ed spotted me crossing an open field and caught me. He sold me to the hunters and made them promise to take me far away." Billy remembered hearing about Elder leaving the colony, but everyone had thought he had found his way to a new home. Billy now knew more than ever, that Farmer Ed was deadly serious about getting rid of all the beavers from his land.

When they finally arrived back at Happy Valley, the other beavers shouted, "We told you that Impossible Creek couldn't be dammed!" But they were happy to see Elder safe and sound, and when they heard the story of the escape, they were grateful to Billy and Chewie.

LEARNING COMPANION 14

Conversation Points: Attitude

By saving Elder and keeping a cool head while being chased by the hunters, Billy demonstrates his command of yet another success principle... a **Positive Mental Attitude** (PMA). This is the right attitude for each set of circumstances that you encounter.

PMA is made up of elements such as **Faith** (the unwavering belief in something or that something you desire will happen), **Integrity** (living up to your word), and other characteristics such as **Optimism, Courage, Initiative, Generosity, Tolerance, Tact, Kindness** and good ole' **Common Sense.** Look these words up in a dictionary so that you are crystal clear as to what they mean. Start practicing these qualities and make them part of you.

In this chapter Billy demonstrates a **Just Do It**, or **Keep Moving Forward** (KMF) attitude in response to the hunters. A great affirmation is **Do something when you think of it.** By seizing the moment to do something that needs to be done you can save valuable time and energy. Have you ever avoided changing a burned out light bulb? By tending to it when you first see it instead of waiting to do it later, you might just avoid the fall in the dark that comes when those stairs aren't well lit. You also avoid the wasted time and energy that comes with thinking about it every time you pass the burned out bulb. This is called, **Removing a Tolerance**, a significant success principle. You can proceed more effectively with your bigger purpose when you are clear of all the tolerances by saying, "I'm going to fix or complete... (whatever the tolerance is at the time, e.g. change a light bulb, or fix a cracked stair), allowing me to focus on my MDP." It also keeps that greatest of all computers, the mind, defragged. This is the computer term for an organized memory where data is organized and useless information has been deleted.

Billy also acted quickly. He assessed the situation and then quickly decided to save Elder. **Some people get stuck when they try to look at all the angles instead of taking action.** As we have learned, this is called, Paralysis by Analysis, and it can keep you from taking any action at all. If Billy had hesitated too long, by over planning the escape, he might have lost his opportunity to save Elder. A magical way of saying this is, "There is a postage-stamp-sized opportunity—a brief moment when one can make a leap of action."

The other Beavers, although they laughed at Billy's visit to Impossible Creek, were grateful to Billy. Gratitude is an important principle to experience as you start and end your day, and in between.

We can sense an opening of possibility for the colony to help Billy achieve his dream.

Write, reflect and discuss…

_____
_____
_____
_____
_____
_____
_____
_____
_____
_____
_____
_____
_____
_____
_____
_____
_____
_____

Knowledge Nugget!

You can't control how others feel about you.

Billy learns a lesson after sharing his goal of creating a new home. He will learn that he cannot control how anyone else feels about him, such as other beavers laughing at his quest. He did not hide his desire to take his adventure, initially on his own, without any thought or fear of making his fellow beavers jealous or uncomfortable in other ways.

Possibility Pond

Learning Points: Positive Mindset

Sometimes, on our journey to our goals, unrelated events can play an important role in our quest. Often these opportunities don't seem connected to our quest, but in time we find out that they are. These opportunities appear for brief moments in time, as did Billy's chance to save Elder. Being open to these life-changing opportunities often requires a clear mind. Billy was able to hide effectively in the forest because his fur blended in well with the surroundings. Beavers must tend to their fur each day if it is to remain healthy and clean. If Billy had procrastinated about cleaning his fur, he might have been discovered and trapped. In life, it is a good idea to get rid of tolerances in the moment they present themselves, like changing that burned out light bulb. Billy having light-coloured woodchips in his fur could have spelled disaster if he hadn't taken care of it immediately.

Helping Elder has added to the strength of his Major Definite Purpose (MDP) to find a new home. It is now a life or death proposition for him and his colony.

Questions

- Do you have a **Positive Mental Attitude**? Look up the meaning of words such as faith, integrity and initiative.

- Do you have the **Just Do It** habit, or do you get mired in extensive analysis of your challenges? If you delay unnecessarily it's called Paralysis by Analysis.

- Do you have any tolerances that are on your **To Do List** that you could do right now?

- Do these tolerances cost you time and waste energy?

- Have you ever experienced a **Postage Stamp of Opportunity**—a moment when you could take positive action? Did you take it, or let it slip by?

Exercise

- Retell this chapter of the story in your own words.

Write, reflect and discuss...

Elder's support convinced other beavers to join Billy's quest.

Chapter 15: Elder Speaks His Truth

All the beavers knew that Billy and Chewie had gone out of their way to save Elder, putting them in grave danger. Elder hadn't said much about the experience as he was still recovering. One day he climbed up to the top of the lodge and smacked his powerful tail, BOOM!

Elder called all the beavers to listen. Everyone stopped talking and wondered what was up. Even though they were tired from the night's work fixing Farmer Ed's damage, they turned and looked up at Elder. Elder shouted, "Billy's dream of damming Impossible Creek is possible! There is food growing all over and there are no people for miles around. This is the chance that we have all been waiting for! I'm going to help him." Elder spoke with passion because he also believed the beavers had to get away from people. He remembered clearly and painfully his long ordeal with the hunters. Some of the beavers were excited by Elder's support of Billy. However, others thought that Elder was delirious from being a prisoner in a small cage for too long.

Billy and Chewie swam home. They shot up through the floor of their lodge like two trained seals and slid, into their room. Just before he fell asleep, Billy imagined his new home on Impossible Creek. He could see the water rising up the sides of the valley as it filled the dam. There were beaver lodges everywhere. He could see moose and elk taking long drinks at the water's edge. He could feel happiness and contentment as he swam and tasted the cool, clear water. As Billy drifted off to sleep, he realized he didn't know how Impossible Creek would be dammed, but he was content in the belief that his dream would happen.

Early the next morning they were awakened by the sound of beavers slapping their tails on the water outside the lodge. They quickly swam through the hole in the floor, and when they came to the surface they were greeted by Elder and some of the other beavers. "We're going with you, Billy." they chorused. Billy was overjoyed and he could see Elder smiling behind them. As Billy swam by, Elder winked in approval. Billy realized that Elder's support convinced the other beavers to join his quest.

Possibility Pond

LEARNING COMPANION 15

Conversation Points: Avoidance

Finally, Billy receives the support he needs to continue with his quest. When Elder speaks out in support of Billy's idea it becomes clear to many in the colony that they need to change their approach and find a new home. Farmer Ed is making life much more difficult than the beavers can handle. His next step will be to use dynamite, which will most likely leave many beavers dead. Happy Valley has outlived its name and, for the first time, many of the beavers realize they must change their behaviour.

Some people resist change, choosing to stay in situations that are no longer healthy for them, long past the point where adversity is a healthy learning. When a situation is no longer working in a healthy and satisfying way, one must seek new options. When change is avoided it is likely that circumstances will be taken out of your hands and the situation will change anyway. However, with the proper application of Success Principles, many people find something much better and have often wondered, "Why didn't I make that change sooner?"

Learning Points: Visualization

In this chapter, **Billy is repaid for his Random Act of Kindness** in helping Elder, when he is finally given the support and recognition he deserves for his ideas. By Going the Extra Mile, Billy receives Elder's support. He, in turn, enlists the support of a few of the other beavers who originally doubted Billy. **Elder has become another member of Billy's Mastermind Alliance.** The members of Billy's MMA are now Billy's subconscious, Chewie and Elder. Before sleeping, Billy does another important activity, he uses his imagination to reinforce his vision, **he reviews his EndPoint Vision in detail.**

Again, Billy imagines that Impossible Creek is dammed. This is a key activity with any goal: to repeatedly visualize a positive outcome. These internal images activate powerful mental software that encourages the subconscious to work on your goal. Planting the seeds of your vision in your subconscious right before you go to sleep is a powerful way to achieve your goals. The next step is to trust in something greater than yourself. Something I trust is Infinite Intelligence. Billy has taken action and practiced many Success Principles, one of which is Faith. He has faith that Infinite Intelligence and his Mastermind Alliance will provide him with the means to reach his goal.

Billy does this by imagining his goal, emotionalizing it, and then letting it go in the knowing that it will happen ... somehow.

It is important to recognize that Elder, the older beaver, has played a most important role in saving the beaver colony. Grandparents can play a similar role in supporting their grandchildren and giving them unconditional love as they go on their quests. Young people today can never have too much love and support, and grandparents can adopt this Love and Support journey as their Major Definite Purpose. Our son, Jeff, affirms the African proverb, "It takes a village to raise a child," today.

Questions

- Have you ever had someone who originally doubted your ideas, finally join in with you? If so, this belief keeps you open to possibility.

- What changed their mind?

- Are you resisting changing something in your life that obviously doesn't work?

- Have you visualized your goals in detail? Do you review your EndPoint Vision before you go to bed each night?

- Do you use affirmations, or positive statements worded in the present tense, that acknowledges that the goal has been achieved? For example Billy's could be, "I am living in a beautiful lodge in a pristine pond." This is an application of integrity; when you always keep your word, then you can live now as though the desired goal has been achieved. The 9/11 affirmations described in the Learning Companion for chapter 4, build integrity. Parents and grandparents can help the young people build their 9/11 program for success.

- Do you trust Infinite Intelligence to help you accomplish your goals by thinking about your requests and then being grateful when they have come about?

- Do you expect help from unexpected places? Faith in the success of your goal keeps you open to this possibility.

Exercise

- Retell this chapter of the story in your own words.

Knowledge Nugget!

The 4 Agreements (+1), by Miguel Ruiz

When embarking on a journey such as Billy and his MMA are undertaking, one needs much guidance to successfully work with many others of diverse ages and backgrounds. Miguel Ruiz, author of the best-selling book, *The 4 Agreements,* offers succinct guidance for leading or being part of such an endeavor:

1. Be impeccable with your word. (self & others)

The definition of impeccable includes, holding to the highest standards, faultless. When you are impeccable with your word you are honest, have integrity and are not afraid to say you don't know. Billy's MMA operates from the place of being impeccable, meaning they can all count on each other to be honest and do the best they can.

2. Do not take anything personally.

Billy, Chewie and Elder are not able (at this time) to solve the challenge posed by stopping the fast-flowing stream. They are doing their best and they have not been successful yet. By practicing, "Don't take anything personally", any negative comments do not impact them and they are able to focus on their goal.

3. Do not make assumptions.

That is required for the participants of any MMA. Clarifying communication you are not sure of is most important. Billy checked again with Willy to confirm his directions to Impossible Creek were clear.

4. Always do your best.

You may not feel the same from one day to the next, but always do the best you can. Elder will demonstrate this attribute when, at some risk, he continues to chew at the base of the tree to ensure that it falls correctly.

5. Be Skeptical. (Ruiz added this one later)

It seemed to be common knowledge among the beavers that this creek was not able to be dammed. By using the 5th agreement, Billy was able to consider other options and chose to attempt to dam Impossible Creek. This agreement is great advice in today's world where we are overloaded with information on the internet and social media. It seems that you can find information to support any perspective, positive or negative, leaving out the critical activity of checking the facts. Billy chose to be skeptical of the opinions of others and test the waters for himself.

Write, reflect and discuss…

Billy did not have any thought of giving up. "There must be a way," he whispered to the world.

Chapter 16: Changing Impossible to Possible

It wasn't long before the team of beavers arrived at Impossible Creek. They cut down trees of all sizes, stopping now and then to snack on tender poplar branches. Some of them moved large logs toward the creek.

Others built ditches that filled with water so that they could drag and float even larger trees to the water's edge. Toward the end of the day, they had built a dam on two sides of the creek. They were now ready to join the two sides of the dam together to block Impossible Creek. But, as they dragged heavy logs to the opening in the dam, the rushing water swept the logs away, just as it had done when Billy and Chewie tried.

Over and over they attempted to close the dam but nothing seemed to work. The beavers turned to Elder. He was the oldest and the wisest; surely he would know what to do. But Elder just shook his head and sighed, "I can't think of anything, I don't know what to do!" The beavers' happiness quickly changed to frustration. Suddenly they all felt tired and dejected. It was the end of a long day for all of them.

Billy and Chewie crawled into a hollow tree to sleep. Billy was exhausted. "What can I do?" he asked himself. He was surprised that he did not feel angry or sad. He was also surprised that Egor wasn't back gloating about the apparent disaster. Billy didn't have thoughts of giving up. "There must be a way to join the dam together somehow," he whispered to the world.

Billy lay back on the soft pine needles and looked up at the beautiful, harvest moon rising over the fir trees. The soft, warm moonlight was reflected in his rich brown fur. Chewie was already asleep and breathing softly in dreamland. An old spider web shimmered in the moonlight reminding him of an Ojibwe dream catcher. Billy smiled to himself and said "Dream catcher, dream catcher, catch me a dream. Give me the answer to damming the stream." With that he closed his heavy eyelids and drifted off to sleep.

LEARNING COMPANION 16

Conversation Points: Darkness

Billy is clearly pursuing his Major Definite Purpose of building a new home away from humans. He finally has a supportive Mastermind Alliance and he has gone the Extra Mile by helping Elder. He defeated Egor by controlling his own mind, and has stayed positive. Yet, he is still encountering adversity. At this point, some would give up and say, "We have come this far, and for what? All our efforts have been for nothing." **It is at times like this, the darkest time in the quest, that a true Mastermind Alliance is critical.** If Billy is surrounded by individuals who are positive, supportive and solution oriented, he will be able to stay focused. If others complain and point out all the reasons why they are failing, Billy's chances of finding a solution will be diminished. Notice that the voice of Egor has all but disappeared at this point. **Billy has managed to gain control of his own mind.** Now he must direct his attention toward a positive outcome and ignore any negative feedback from others.

What Billy needs at this time is creative problem solving. None of the other beavers came up with an idea, not even Elder. Billy trusts that the solution is to be found in his dreams, something so many creative individuals have discovered to be fruitful. The indigenous Ojibwe people knew the power of dreams, as did people like Einstein, who imagined riding a sunbeam to get his theory of relativity that changed the world, and musicians such as John Lennon who created the song *Imagine* from a dream. Often, we get clues and answers in our dreams when we clearly pose questions to Infinite Intelligence before we go to sleep. **Be sure to put a pad of paper by your bed to write down the answers from your dreams.** This will help you train yourself to listen to the messages that can be found in your dreams.

Questions

- List some of the big obstacles you have encountered.
- Have you ever met a big obstacle to a goal and given up?
- Did you ever reframe a challenge and go on to succeed?
- Do you ever get ideas from your dreams? Maybe you get them while you are doing something else. Many people get ideas in the shower.

Write, reflect and discuss…

Knowledge Nugget!

Our greatest fears arise because of the unknown.

Our challenge is to continually adapt to change. When we take on a new project, the effort required causes much change. Handling the types of change and associated uncertainty that arise is an important understanding for all of us to have.

Possibility Pond

Learning Points: Problem Solving

During the times when your desired goal faces its strongest barriers, it is a good idea to stop and review your progress and to **express gratitude**. By recognizing your progress, and being thankful for your current position, you keep your mind focused on the positive, and therefore it works much better.

Billy has **a great MMA** and he has achieved much by continuing to **Keep Moving Forward (KMF)** in the face of adversity. He has also managed to keep a **Positive Attitude**. This simplifies the problem by not having too many things to worry about. Instead of saying, "The stream is frustrating our efforts," he can reframe the situation and say, "The dam is almost built. All we have to do is join the sides together." Re-framing challenges in a positive way is a useful skill to develop. It helps to keep the mind open to possibility and creative solutions. Billy needs a creative solution, but none of the beavers seem able to look past the obvious.

One method to generate creative solutions is brainstorming, coming up with many ideas no matter how crazy they seem. The process asks you to repeatedly come up with many divergent ideas and then relate them back to the challenge. Next, you select a few that show promise (converging) and begin to brainstorm again (diverging). This process can be repeated several times. In this way, many possibilities are considered that may seem unlikely and unsuccessful until explored to this depth. Mind mapping is a form of generating creative solutions. By creating a web of ideas that branch out from a central defining point, new options are considered. There is much written on this method and it is easily researched on the internet.

Another method is to ask for help from Infinite Intelligence. By clearly asking for help from the dream catcher, Billy has activated his subconscious to search for answers and has reinforced his belief that a response will come.

Exercise

- Retell this chapter of the story in your own words.

- Create a mind map to structure ideas that come up when you brainstorm, for example:

- Brainstorm as many solutions to Billy's challenge as you can. All ideas are valid. Do not reject wild ideas; they often lead to solutions. If you are still stuck for ideas, try **Reverse the Obvious**: think of ideas to make it NOT work. This may surface new ideas that create a solution. These ideas will cause you to look at things differently and will trigger fresh ideas.

Write, reflect and discuss...

___

Knowledge Nugget!

The Magic of Mind Mapping

We encourage you to learn to mind map. Some of the uses are its ability to facilitate green-lighting a plan of action, which is coming up with many ideas in a free flow, evaluating them and then selecting the good ones. Another application is to create a mind map of a talk, you wish to give. Use icons or hand drawn pictures to help you remember your talking points. In this way, the next point can be loaded into your brain with a quick glance during the presentation.

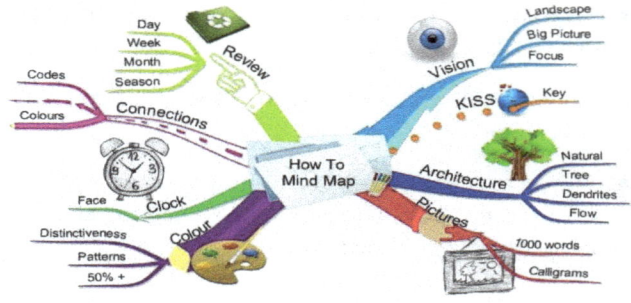

Image source: Wikimedia.org, Creative Commons Licence

As he continued to dream, Billy felt closer to the spider

Chapter 17: The Gift of Being Calm

Later that night Billy had a dream about Willy the spider. It seemed so realistic, he felt as though he was back in Willy's cave. Billy remembered the spider pointing the way to Impossible Creek during their first meeting. He wondered if Willy had caught more bugs in his new web.

As he continued to dream, Billy felt closer to the spider, and felt silly that he had been afraid of Willy at all. He remembered how scared he was as he watched Willy building his silky web, and how afraid he felt being alone in the forest, so far from home. In his dream, Billy saw how the spider let out his web and watched as the silk drifted in the wind toward his face, like the tentacle of an octopus. Luckily the silk thread had missed him and stuck to the opposite side of Willy's cave. This created an anchor line and gave Willy a bridge so he could cross the open space of the cave to finish his web.

Billy woke up and shouted, "That's it! I know how we can dam Impossible Creek!" Billy's dream reminded him of a huge fir tree standing beside the creek. Beavers don't like eating fir trees because they have so much sticky sap, so the beavers hadn't thought of using that tree as part of the dam.

As well, that tree is much larger than any of the poplar trees, and certainly bigger than any tree a beaver had ever cut down. Just as Willy had done with his silk thread, this tree could be used like an anchor line if they could just cut it down.

"That's all we have to do, chew through the fir tree and drop it across the opening in the dam!" yelled Billy. "And it won't be swept away; it's too heavy!"

Possibility Pond

LEARNING COMPANION 17

Conversation Points: Impossibility

Even though Billy has done a great job following Success Principles, the beavers encounter yet another adversity. Billy does a marvellous job at keeping his mind positive so he can focus on a solution to the problem.

He is certainly under pressure to perform, given that many beavers have come a long way to assist him. When he goes to sleep, instead of his mind being preoccupied with doubts, fears, and stress which would prohibit his going to solution, Billy is clear about his challenge. He has asked for guidance and is ready to listen for clues.

In the documentary film Free Solo, Alex Hannold feels the pressure when moving toward the day he will free-climb the 3200-foot vertical granite face of El Capitan in Yosemite National Park. Yet, he has the courage to delay his climb by a full year, as he has several key steps that he must create, and others to enhance. He is confident that his Mastermind Alliance film crew will understand. They are his allies.

In his relaxed state, Billy dreams about his encounter with Willy, something other than his immediate problem. Often solutions come when you are thinking about something else, instead of trying to force a solution. There is a sense that he is confident in receiving the answer. When Billy gets the clue from his dream, he practices a creative problem solving technique called thinking outside of the box. He considers something that has never been tried before. He takes two unrelated concepts, a spider's web and a beaver dam, and creatively links them, producing an entirely new solution to the problem. (On his El Capitan climb, Alex decides to use an innovative Karate kick instead of a conventional jump to traverse a challenging portion of the climb.)

Billy is considering using a fir tree, a type of wood that beavers don't like to eat. Not only does Billy think of cutting down a type of tree that beavers don't usually touch, he thinks of cutting down a REALLY BIG tree…bigger than any other tree the beavers have cut down.

Learning Points: Genius

In this chapter Billy demonstrates some of the qualities of a genius. One of the challenges often faced when taking on a major goal, is that we don't think that we have the ability to accomplish our goal. Billy doesn't feel like a genius or look like a genius to the other beavers, nevertheless, he has many of the characteristics of a genius, that is, a lot of ability to succeed.

In today's rapidly changing world, many people, both young and old, feel unqualified and lacking in ability. The author has successfully used the list of characteristics of a genius to evaluate and encourage individuals to pursue their interests. This process helps them discover they have more skills than they recognize.

There are many negatives for people seeking a career path today. The book *The Death of an Artist: How Creators are Struggling to Survive in the Age of Billionaires and Big Tech*, by William Deresiewicz, is an example of a negative possibility that can change an individual's resolve to follow their dream. The author of *Possibility Pond* used the Characteristics of a Genius to build the confidence of one of his sons, showing him that he had all the skills required to qualify as a genius, and who subsequently has become very successful. The crowning benefit is that he loves what he does.

Use "Characteristics of a Genius" on the next page to assess Billy. Does he possess these characteristics?

Questions

- Can you think of other out of the box solutions to Billy's challenge?

- Do you consider yourself a genius by the characteristics described in the next section, Learning Points? Run through the list and give reasons for your decisions.

- What personal gift do you possess that is unique to you, and defines your own brand of genius? Don't be shy!

- Have you ever solved a problem in your dreams?

- Can you think of a solution to a challenge you are facing that requires you to connect two unrelated ideas or situations?

"If you can't get beyond your stresses, your problems, and your pain, you cannot create a new future." -- Joe Dispenza, *Becoming Supernatural*

For Billy, this was another place for his colony and him to live. Notice he didn't say, "Let's find another river or pond." Instead, he is working hard to make it possible for Impossible Creek to become a liveable home. Having lots of the success principle of Determination is required.

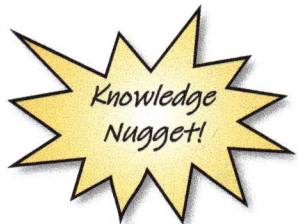
Knowledge Nugget!

Reflections on the Definition of Genius.

My wife Sandy and I took a remarkable course by Dr. Joe Dispenza, author of the best-selling books, "You are the Placebo, Breaking the Habit of Being Yourself, and Becoming Supernatural." We confirmed with previous graduates, that this course was positively life-changing and felt it was an opportunity we wanted to experience. One belief Dispenza is absolutely crystal clear about, and expresses to course participants early on, is that his students are geniuses.

This statement left me feeling a little false as I did not consider myself of genius status, especially when I compared myself to the likes of Albert Einstein who I felt was of true genius calibre. On reflection, I realized that when I applied the definition of success based on Napoleon Hill's work on Billy, the results concluded that he was a genius.

When I applied these same Success Principle genius characteristics to myself I discovered that I too was a genius. I came away understanding that the definition of genius is much broader than I had ever thought. This enabled me to embrace the upcoming course with confidence and excitement.

Take a moment to do this exercise for yourself in some significant area that you are working on. You will come away with much more confidence that indeed you have the skills necessary to accomplish your goals, your own brand of genius. You may also learn what skills you need to develop to improve your success. Win, win! You might apply this activity to a loved one or friend who is embarking on a significant undertaking. By learning this definition of genius, you and those in your life will begin to see that a genius encompasses so much more that what we have been led to believe.

Many think of a Genius as someone who has completed significant mathematical work or the like. However, there are people who have made major discoveries and had great successes and who had been classified as not that gifted. These days people are challenged with uncertainty and change, especially youth. When our genius characteristics are identified, it is much easier to move forward, having the knowledge of Success Principles to support our journeys in life.

Characteristics of a Genius: Applied to Billy

1. **Definiteness of Purpose** - Billy wants to find a new home away from humans, a Major Definite Purpose.

2. **Applied Faith** - He has faith that he will find a solution to damming Impossible Creek.

3. **Enthusiasm** - It was Billy's enthusiasm that convinced Chewie to support him and join his Mastermind Alliance.

4. **Imagination** - Billy demonstrates he has the ability to come up with new ideas, like looking for a home away from humans and using the fir tree to form an anchor bridge across the dam.

5. **Motivation** - Billy has continued past many adversities to reach his goal.
   There are at least ten motivators Napoleon Hill outlined; Billy is driven by the following five:

   - **Self Preservation**: he wants to survive
   - **Love**: he would love a pristine pond
   - **Fear**: of Farmer Ed, and of criticism
   - **Freedom of body and mind**: he wants his own pond and lodge
   - **Material Gain**: he will have all the food he needs

   The other five motivators are:

   - **Hate**
   - **Revenge**
   - **Life after death**
   - **Sex**
   - **Recognition**

   It is valuable to know them and to memorize them, and use them as a checklist as to why you want to accomplish a goal.

6. **Personal Initiative followed by action** - He started on the journey himself and has not stopped.

7. **Go the Extra Mile** - He went out of his way to save Elder, even though he had worked hard that day, and had traveled a long way.

8. **A Mastermind Alliance** - He has formed a Mastermind Alliance with himself, Chewie and Elder and has a team of beavers supporting him.

9. **A Positive Attitude** - This is evident. We can only conclude that Billy has all of the attributes of a genius

Possibility Pond

Learning Points continued...

When my son Luke was experiencing doubt about his ability to achieve his challenging Major Definite Purpose, I suggested he explore the characteristics of a genius. By reviewing these success qualities, he came to understand that he did have what was required, and he moved forward with enthusiasm and inspiration. He found the necessary belief in himself. It was a life changing exercise. Today he enjoys amazing success living his dream.

Exercise

- Retell this chapter of the story in your own words.

Write, reflect and discuss...

Knowledge Nugget!

We can only envision items we have the descriptive language for.

It is my belief that you cannot think a thought, unless you have the words to describe it. This is a powerful idea. In the Learning Points, there are many valuable words and expressions to assist you in describing how you may evaluate your progress. They can be used as an effective checklist. You now have a functional definition of the word Genius, meaning the ability you require to succeed in your endeavor.

When this tree falls across Impossible Creek it will join the banks, just like a spider web between two branches.

Chapter 18: Billy Trusts His Vision

Billy leapt up before daybreak and moved quickly from the shelter of the hollow tree. He knew the key to building the dam was that big fir tree. If it fell just right, it would be like the first strong strand of silk that Willy had used to weave his web across the cave opening,

But how can it be made to fall just right?

The sound of frantic gnawing on wood woke the other beavers. Looking around to see what was causing the sound, they saw Billy chewing at the base of a monstrous tree. Running up to investigate, they cried, "What are you doing?" Billy turned and they saw his mouth was full of sticky wood chips, as thick as shaving cream. Another beaver spoke, "Billy, that tree is too old and tough to eat and it's way too big to move." Billy, who had already been chewing for hours, spit the wood chips out of his mouth and responded excitedly saying, "If we cut this tree down, no, what I mean is, WHEN this tree falls on Impossible Creek, it will join the dam, just like a spider builds a web between two distant branches." The beavers looked at each other in bewilderment. "What do spiders and dams have in common?" they asked in unison. Billy explained what he had learned by watching Willy build his web, a seemingly impossible task. "All a spider needs to do is get that first line of silk across an opening, and then the rest is easy. We can do the same with the fir tree!" said Billy with conviction.

Possibility Pond

LEARNING COMPANION 18

Conversation Points: Diffusion

When you have a Mastermind Alliance working together on a goal, one person tends to be the Keeper of the Vision, often the originator of the idea. In this story that is Billy. Although Elder is older, wiser and stronger than Billy in many ways, he is unable to come up with a solution for damming Impossible Creek. Having a Major Definite Purpose, Billy has certain advantages. His mind remains alert and open to new possibilities and he has the motivation to keep moving forward. Now he combines this with making decisions quickly so he can build more self-confidence.

Many people don't take action when they are not sure. However, this is the time to take action, ANY ACTION! It is easy to change something; it is darn hard to change nothing. Taking action leads to new understandings and fresh insights that will lead to a solution, often one that you really did not expect. So be open to solutions coming from unexpected sources. Initially, Billy is unable to solve this tough challenge, and he asks for help. The help comes when he relaxes and waits expectantly for an answer. Billy has Faith in his Major Definite Purpose and TRUSTS that somehow, he will find an answer. As the keeper of the vision, all these traits give Billy superior problem-solving ability.

Many of the greatest minds in the world acknowledge an unseen force they call Infinite Intelligence, that provides information and solutions to challenges.

Although they are his biggest supporters, neither Chewie nor Elder has devoted as much time and energy to Billy's goal as he has, so it is not surprising that Billy is the one that comes up with the solution. He has the passion, the vision, and has already taken purposeful action toward solving the challenge. Damming Impossible Creek is a huge step in achieving his MDP and he devotes all his energy to this goal.

Question and Exercise

- Have you ever had an idea about solving a challenge that other people thought was crazy? It requires you to have the strength of your convictions.

- Try the magnifying glass exercise: Take a magnifying glass and a piece of paper and focus the light from the sun on the paper in as intense a beam as you can, but in a safe environment. You will start seeing smoke and then the paper will catch fire. What happens when you do not keep the glass steady? Nothing! This is similar to the result you get when you don't focus on your goal, and you spread your energy and attention to many areas.

Write, reflect and discuss...

Knowledge Nugget!

Place Yourself Inside the Story

To form memories, the reader and the listener need to imagine being participants in the story. This engages the senses, emotions and imagination. You connect to the story as your own. There is much activity going on in this part of the story that you can connect with. Just take action and do it!

Success principles can be used to describe what is taking place, and to analyze whether the factors in your efforts are good ones.

Possibility Pond

Conversation Points continued...

One success formula is: Vision + Passion + Purposeful Action + Mastermind Alliance = SUCCESS

Billy demonstrates an application of the success formula in this chapter.

Pursuing a Major Definite Purpose with passion seems to enhance one's personal powers and connection to the Infinite Intelligence. In Billy's case these are:

- **Self-reliance:**
  The ability to take care of one's self especially on your MDP journey.

- **Personal Initiative:**
  Taking action with you as the starter.

- **Imagination:**
  Thinking of and envisioning many possibilities.

- **Enthusiasm:**
  A sense of spirit within you that sheds sunlight on everything you work on.

- **Self-discipline:**
  Delaying gratification, not becoming diverted from the goal by frivolous things that may provide satisfaction in the short term.

- **Concentration of effort:**
  By attending to key actions you avoid becoming scattered and unable to accomplish anything.

- **Focus:**
  The ability to keep your attention and energy on the task.

Learning Points: Focus

Billy's steady focus on his goal has the same effect as a magnifying glass channeling a beam of sunlight. Using a magnifying glass, you can focus the sunlight on one point and start a fire. Billy's concentration of effort on one goal has a similar effect; sooner or later this will build up enough energy to attract enough support to accomplish his goal. And, like the magnifying glass, Billy must keep his lens, his mind, focused on his goal. If he constantly changes his focus, he won't build up the necessary momentum to accomplish his goal.

Exercise

- Retell this chapter of the story in your own words. Consider adding personal experiences to illustrate the message.

Knowledge Nuggets!

Repetition Makes a Miracle of the Mind

When remembering and learning new material, the Celtic people of Ireland said, "Repetition makes a miracle of the mind." A similar expression I also like is "Repetition is the mother of learning." In some cases you will learn bit by bit, and it may be slow, but we are always looking for ways to strengthen memory. The method that follows in one important exercise to do just that.

Icons: Visual Symbols Spark Learning and Recall

In this section, you've been given a formula for achieving success. You were advised to participate and, take action. An excellent idea is to create pictures or icons of the material. For example, to remember the formula for success, you may create icons for each part of the formula such as: an eye for vision, a heart for passion, a person running for Purposeful Action. Napoleon Hill believed that your mind becomes more powerful when you have an MMA and when the members of the MMA are working in perfect harmony. This can be represented by an icon of a group of people working together and creating a larger, shared problem solving mind. A mountain with a flag can represent a successful result.

Draw your own Success Formula icons:

Transmutation is a Change of State

This action of changing the word description of the success formula described above, into icons, is called transmutation. The act of creating a picture to replace the word (or words) improves your ability to remember an idea. Transmutation also means "the action of changing the state of something into another form" such as turning lead into gold. This a great method for improving understanding, memory and recall.

Possibility Pond

The power of a Mastermind Alliance: Elder was the first to move forward to help Billy.

Chapter 19: Leading by Example

Elder was the first to step forward and offer to help Billy. He was bigger and more powerful than most of the beavers, despite his long stay in captivity. With each bite he chomped off a massive chunk of the fir tree. He paused for a moment, considering the task at hand.

Then Elder said, "We must chew more of the tree away on the stream side so that it will fall in the water and not on the shore." Billy and the other beavers had never thought of that possibility.

Usually beavers begin chewing at the base of a tree and then go round and round as they chew. The tree may fall in any direction, perhaps the way the wind was blowing that day. Trees that beavers cut down are usually small, and once felled, can be easily cut into logs and moved to where they are needed. Or if a tree is too big, it only serves as food. Once the bark is eaten it would be left where it fell. This big fir tree was different. Once it came down they wouldn't be able to move it. It had to fall exactly where they needed it.

Elder began to chew with purpose. Soon, there was only a little bit of wood left holding the gigantic tree up and it began to shudder. Like a huge giant who has lost his balance, the tree appeared to be struggling to regain control.

It swayed slightly one way and then another, seeming as though it could fall in any direction. At Elder's command, the beavers dashed to the side of the tree away from the stream and started pushing it toward the rushing water. Being close to such a large tree when it fell was dangerous for the beavers, but they had to make sure the tree fell the right way. Once it landed, there would be no moving it.

Possibility Pond

72

LEARNING COMPANION 19

Conversation Points: Wisdom

This chapter demonstrates the power of a great Mastermind Alliance. Billy has the pivotal idea about using the fir tree, but it is Elder's wisdom that makes it work. By valuing and being open to Elder's experience, a key person in his Mastermind Alliance, Billy's vision has a better chance of being successful. An important characteristic to develop in life is to respect the wisdom of your Elders. People who have lived longer than us can often play a critical role in our success, all we need to do is ask for their help and then listen. So many times, the Elders around us are not considered for their life experiences and wisdom or worse, they are forgotten. By tapping into this incredible resource, you can get that much closer to achieving your MDP.

Whenever you are asking for assistance, remember to find people who support your ideas, and with their guidance you can make informed decisions. Avoid seeking help from people who tend to see all the roadblocks instead of the possibilities. These individuals are not good candidates for your Mastermind Alliance. Billy put his vision aside when he helped Elder escape the hunters. His willingness to then follow Elder's guidance increased Billy's chances of success. Remember, it was Elder who finally convinced many of the other beavers to join Billy's quest.

As much as you will rely on the ideas and support of your MMA, it is important to keep in mind that you are 100% responsible for any decisions that you make. The members of your MMA are there to inspire, advise, provide ideas and experience to support your MDP. Billy considered Elder's suggestion about how best to chew the fir tree and ultimately agreed with his idea. By taking responsibly for the decisions he makes, Billy avoids falling into the blame game, and remains in control of his vision.

Questions

- Can you think of times when you have been given advice by an Elder that helped you in your life?
- Do you most often listen to your Elders, or do you tend to ignore them?
- Have you ever been in a situation where you had to place yourself in danger to reach a goal?
- Think of some of the dreams that you have had. What has stopped you from achieving them?
- Consider a goal you have at this time and identify what motivates you to achieve it.

The Joy of Expressive Synonyms

In later sections, you will be asked to express the Success Principles using different or fewer words. This helps strengthen your memory of the concept. A success attribute I value and wish to share is curiosity. Using a thesaurus site such as wordhippo.com, you can find synonyms to express the same or similar meaning. Wordhippo.com offers 30 alternatives for the work "curiosity". Here are 5 that I liked: inquisitiveness, inquiring mind, questioning, snoopiness, a desire for knowledge. I love the word curious, since I think of myself as curious George the monkey, and use that name often when introducing myself, so people will remember who I am. This habit allowed curiosity to become an affirmation for me which reinforces my habit of acting this way: I am willing to explore most aspects of life where possible. By finding other descriptors, there are now new ways to express an idea and enhance your learning!

Write, reflect and discuss…

_____
_____
_____
_____
_____
_____
_____
_____

Transform Adversity into Opportunity

Your adversity quotient (AQ) is important in our turbulent, changing world. This is the ability to transform adversity into opportunity. I would give Billy at least a nine out of 10. Where are you in this regard? Assign a value and work to improve it. Most new discoveries come from dealing with adversity. It causes you to think of new ideas and solutions.

Possibility Pond

Learning Points: Motivation

As a result of Elder's continued support of Billy, the beavers are willing to act outside the box, that is, try something they have never done before and break from the usual tree cutting habits they were accustomed to. They agree to cut a tree that would gum-up their teeth, and to cut it in such a way that there would be considerable danger when the tree falls. Fear is an important motivator in this story. It is what initially motivates Billy to search for a new home without humans nearby. In this chapter, the beavers must press beyond their fear, cut the fir tree strategically, and push it in the right direction. There are 7 basic fears Napoleon Hill outlined that can motivate our actions:

- Old Age
- Poverty
- Death
- Ill Health
- Criticism
- Loss of Liberty
- Loss of Love

Billy is driven by several of these fears during his quest. He is certainly afraid that Farmer Ed will eventually destroy his home, himself and his fellow beavers. He has been afraid of criticism from the other beavers about his dream and he is concerned about loss of liberty because of Farmer Ed and other humans.

It is important to identify your big WHY in the early stages of your journey. This motivator for striving to achieve your MDP will keep going in the face of adversity. It is also important to have the members of your MMA identify what is motivating them and to consider what gains they will receive by supporting you and your MDP. By understanding what motivates you and your MMA, it will be easier to remain focused on the vision.

Draw Your Own Icons to Anchor the Story

You've been given a formula for succeeding. Another characteristic required for success is wisdom. Through his longer lived life, Elder has determined how to make a tree fall in the desired direction. Add an icon to the success formula to represent this, for example, a stump with the chopped down tree, pointing in the right direction can represent wisdom in this story. Another more general icon would be a head with a question mark in it. Notice that when you change your ideas into icons or pictures they do not need to be works of art, but meaningful. Simplicity can be thought of as an advanced art. By developing your imagination you are creating an important asset for yourself.

Draw the True North Stump that represents Wisdom:

Draw icons to represent the 7 fears:

Old Age

Poverty

Death

Ill Health

Criticism

Loss of Liberty

Loss of Love

Learning Points continued...

Including fear, the 11 motivators are:

1. **Self-preservation**: survival, to thrive

2. **Love**: for a truth or a principle (e.g. Martin Luther King's, "All men are created equal."), love of what you are doing, or the love for another

3. **Fear**: the 7 fears previously discussed

4. **Sex**: the physical expression of love

5. **Life after death**: the belief that there is something to live for beyond this life

6. **Freedom of body and mind**: e.g. be your own boss; be in charge of your destiny

7. **Hate**: to be motivated by or against something you feel negative about

8. **Revenge**: the best expression of revenge is to only get even in a positive way with the people who help you.

9. **Self-expression**: the freedom to say and do what you wish; keep in mind the principle of Do no Harm to Others: Do unto others as they would prefer to have done unto them.

10. **Recognition**: to be seen, understood, acknowledged or appreciated

11. **Material gain**: e.g. money, and considering the use that money will be put to

Of these motivators, it is interesting to note that the top three are: love, sex and material gain.

Although identifying what is motivating you is an important step to success, it is also critical that you believe in the rightness of your dream and have the faith and determination to make it happen. Recognizing the role persistence plays is also an important key to your success.

Even if the big fir tree did not fall and join the two sides of the dam, with the presence of persistence, the beavers could consider other ideas to solve the problem. One option would be to find another large tree to block the river with.

Exercises

- Retell this chapter of the story in your own words. Feel free to add your own thoughts.

- We are a picture processing species, and we readily remember images. Can you create an icon for the adversity quotient?

Transmutation or the changing of one form into another, such as text into icons, is a valuable skill for memorizing and summarizing concepts. Draw icons for the 11 motivators:

Self-preservation

Love

Fear

Sex

Life after death

Freedom

Hate

Revenge

Self-expression

Recognition

Material gain

Knowledge Nugget!

Fail More to Learn More

Napoleon Hill named 7 basic fears. Think of others you may have. I was motivated by a fear of failure to achieve a university degree, and it did not incapacitate me. Instead, it prompted me to study hard. This is a good reminder when those feelings arise. Space-X launched expensive rockets they knew would fail, but were not sure how. This made development occur more rapidly, as they quickly identified areas that needed work. An icon that represents failure could be a tree stump, with the tree falling in the wrong direction or a crashing rocket.

Billy went quickly to Elder's ear and whispered, "You'll be okay. You'll be okay!"

Chapter 20: Staying Present During a Journey

All the beavers pushed together to make the tree fall toward the stream. As the tree began to move, they held their breath. Would it fall the right way? As the tree teetered in the wind, Billy yelled to Chewie and slapped his tail frantically on the ground, "Run Chewie! Run!"

Billy didn't want his sister to be crushed under the tree. Elder stopped pushing for a moment and went around to the other side and chewed a bit more of the tree on the stream side hoping that it would fall in that direction. Elder was placing himself in great danger.

The massive tree began to fall. They all watched, not daring to breathe, and wondered where it would finally come to rest.

When trees fall, they often kick back before they come to rest. This could kill one of the beavers if they were too close to the base of the tree. They scrambled away as fast as they could. As the tree hit the ground, the floor of the forest shuddered like it had been hit by an earthquake. The water in Impossible Creek was thrown into the air, as if a giant whale had landed with a great splash after leaping high.

From a small clearing near the tree stump, the beavers looked anxiously to see where the tree had fallen. As the mist and dust settled, they saw that the big fir tree had landed where they had hoped! They all watched anxiously as the fast-flowing waters of Impossible Creek rushed and pushed against the tree. Impossible Creek wanted to move that tree out of the way, as it had with the other logs, but the huge tree didn't budge. Everyone started to cheer as the water in Impossible Creek began backing up against the fir tree, slowly forming a pond. "We did it! We did it!" yelled Billy. The other beavers let out a cheer. They all knew they could finish the dam.

Billy looked around for Elder. He couldn't see him anywhere. "Elder!" he screamed, but there was no answer. Billy scrambled toward the base of the huge tree. "Oh, no! Oh, no!" he cried to himself, fearing the worst for Elder. When Billy reached the base of the tree, there was Elder, trapped beneath its huge trunk.

As the tree was falling, Elder had continued to chew to make sure that it fell in exactly the right spot. It had landed on his hind legs and tail and had crushed him into the soft, wet ground.

The tree was too huge for them to move! Billy went quickly to Elder's ear and whispered, "You'll be okay. You'll be okay!" Elder's eyes flickered, and they opened slightly. In a weak voice Elder said, "Thank you for sharing your dream with me Billy, I always believed in you." Elder took another breath and said, "Billy, help others dream their dreams. Encourage them to share their dreams and tell them to keep moving forward to make their dreams happen. Help them have faith in themselves, to believe that their goal is a good one."

Elder fell into unconsciousness, believing he had spoken his last words.

Imagine & Believe: The Seemingly Impossible can be Accomplished if You Take the First Step

Billy learned a most valuable life lesson through their success in cutting the huge tree down. He might have initially thought; they could not chew through such a wide trunk, that stopping the rapidly flowing stream was too complicated and too big of a job, or that he was too small. Egor could generate numerous challenges to throw Billy off his MDP. However, Billy learned that he was capable of bigger things than he ever imagined. He realized that the seemingly impossible can be accomplished if you are willing to take the first step and give it everything you've got. He now firmly believes he can do anything he can 'imagine' and 'believe' possible. He now understands the first important step is to imagine or visualize the goal. By doing so it is being brought into existence in a way that allows him to make a plan of action and move forward. He learned that there is a gift to be able to dream and imagine, to go beyond what seems impossible. This realization of Billy's is also a gift to us.

Possibility Pond

LEARNING COMPANION 20

Conversation Points: Stay the Course

Billy's MDP was clearly defined and strongly supported by his MMA. As a team, they had the faith that Billy's dream could become a reality. When other beavers joined to help, it became more powerful, and more possible.

By applying the same principles that Billy has used along his journey, you too can meet with success and achieve your MDP.

Billy strengthened his EPV by clearly envisioning what his new home and newly created pond would look like. As he visualized his dream, he felt deeply what it would feel like to live in that reality, as if it had already occurred. He was also open to receiving inspiration and ideas from other sources as unlikely as a spider. Billy never lost hope and always looked for answers that supported his vision. He was open to the power of the universe.

With his dream etched in his mind, Billy could express his MDP to his Mastermind Alliance in an inspirational way and they could easily join in the journey to make his goal happen. Elder demonstrated this by Going the Extra Mile and chewing more from the tree as it swayed precariously, putting himself in great danger. He was inspired by Billy and the life he was choosing to follow. Having adopted Billy's MDP, Elder was willing to take risks to help Billy achieve his goal. Elder was not able to move to safety in time and became pinned under the great giant he had helped fell. It is not necessary for a member of an MMA to put themselves in danger, however they should always look for the opportunity to go the extra mile, and may be called upon to take risks that they might not normally attempt.

Questions

- What did you enjoy about this story?
- What concerned you?
- What key messages did you receive from this story?
- How do you see yourself applying the Success Principles?
- Elder's advice to Billy "Help others dream their dream," has become a goal in my life. How can you help others with their dreams?
- Imagine the results in your life and the lives of others as these principles are applied. What impact do you see?

Exercises

- Retell this chapter of the story in your own words.
- Express each of the Success Principles in your own words. Give examples that support your life and/or you have seen in others.
- A wonderful exercise that will help you remember these most important principles is to create an icon, a visual symbol, for each of them. Send your work to the author when you have completed this task if you would like some feedback. His email address is on the copyright page.

  If a picture is worth a thousand words, I believe that a picture, annotated or described by you, is worth at least double that.

- Imagine an icon for the concept expressed by the picture of Elder under the fallen tree with a smile in his face. What success principal could it represent? Draw that icon.

Write, reflect and discuss…

_____
_____
_____
_____
_____
_____
_____
_____

Using Fewer Words Anchors the Mind

In the next sections, you will be asked to express various success principle concepts in very few words. This is an idea that you can use in many places to make ideas easier to remember.

Learning Points: Success Principles

Once Billy had determined what his Major Definite Purpose was, he was continually drawn forward by his desire to make it happen. To achieve one's goal, desire must be present and continually attended to in order to keep the fire of the vision burning bright.

The Success Principles are critical tools to help you thrive in many environments:

1. **A Major Definite Purpose (MDP):** Define the MDP for this story in 10 words or less.

2. **A Mastermind Alliance (MMA):** Name the members of the MMA in the story. Describe their roles as you see them.

3. **Faith (F!):** Where in the story did faith play a critical role?

4. **Go the Extra Mile (GEM):** Give three examples where individual beavers went the extra mile, that is, beyond the ordinary tasks that are usually done.

5. **Personal Initiative (PI):** The ability to assess and initiate independently. Give an example from the story.

6. **Pleasing Personality (PP):** The effect is to cause others to feel happy and satisfied. Who best exhibited this characteristic?

7. **Positive Mental Attitude (PMA):** Give an example of when a PMA was necessary for the success of Billy's journey.

8. **Enthusiasm (E!):** Defined as eager enjoyment, interest, or appeal to others. Give story examples.

9. **Self-Discipline (SD):** The ability to control one's feelings and to overcome one's weaknesses. Where in the story does this occur?

10. **Accurate Thinking (AT):** Give an example of accurate thinking or exact predictions correct in all details. An example of inaccurate thinking was what the colony thought had happened to Elder. If the colony had known the truth, they may have been motivated to find a new home much earlier. Find another example in the story.

11. **Controlled Attention (CA):** Often referred to as concentration, it refers to a capacity to choose what to pay attention to and expand on less. Comment on where this took place in the story.

Exercise

- Express each of the Success Principles as an icon and in your own words(10 words or less). This and the acronym for each will aid memorization of the principles. On a blank sheet or in your journal, expand your knowledge by adding examples or explanations. Add examples where they have influenced your life or someone else's. Use a dictionary and thesaurus to assist you.

Possibility Pond

12. **Teamwork (T!):** The combined action of a group, especially when effective and efficient. You cannot be a success without taking others with you. This statement relates to the presence of an MMA. Where in the story was teamwork important to the success of the project?

13. **Learning From Adversity and Defeat (LFAD):** Lessons you learn from hardships often reveal limiting patterns and beliefs, and highlight skills you didn't see or appreciate before. This powerful shift will increase your self-awareness. You now have a chance to make new choices based on what matters; how you act, think and feel; and what you can or can't do. In the face of adversity, we must step out of our comfort zone and explore untapped potential within ourselves. It is believed, that a high Adversity Quotient (AQ) measuring an ability to overcome adversity, is the most important measure of potential success.

14. **Creative Thinking (CT):** The use of the imagination to generate new ideas; coming up with unique and original solutions to stimulate progress.

15. **Budget Time and Money (BTM):** Time is your life currency; decide carefully how you choose to spend it. Make a list of your most important tasks, and devote time and resources to them.

16. **Health (H!):** It is important to pay attention to self-care and be free from illness or injury. Who sustained injuries in the story?

17. **Cosmic Habit Force (CHF):** The law which makes every living creature, every particle of matter, subject to the influence of its environment. Creating good habits is a strong factor in succeeding

18. **Determination (D!):** Firmness of purpose; think of Winston Churchill and his defense of England.

19. **Persistence (P!):** Continuing firmly in an opinion or a course of action despite difficulty or opposition.

20. **Adaptability to Change (A2C):** Change is one thing that is constant in our lives. By accepting this law, you can become more flexible, adaptable and productive.

The first part of his dream was complete and he could now build his lodge in peace.

Chapter 21: The Vision Becomes Reality

Billy yelled frantically to the other beavers. "Quick! Elder is trapped, we don't have much time, start chewing!" The beavers now had the faith to face the impossible, and began chewing Elder free from this mammoth tree before it drained the life from him.

They poured all their energy into chewing the fir tree once again, this time because Elder's life depended on it. Billy's legs were buckling as he pushed and chewed the tree away from Elder. He kept yelling, "Chew, chew, chew!" With one last effort, the beaver's cut through the tree just enough to slide Elder's body out from underneath its weight.

Billy could see the mist rise from Elder's mouth as he gasped for air and knew that Elder would be okay. With Elder out of danger, the beavers could turn to the building of their new dam.

Now that Impossible Creek was tamed, construction of the dam went quickly. Billy and his friends moved massive amounts of tree trunks, branches, rocks and mud to make the walls of the dam strong. When there was a leak, they moved to patch it. The clear waters of Impossible Creek were forming a beautiful pond. The extra water from the fast, flowing creek tumbled over the massive tree trunk to form a majestic waterfall. The sound of the falling water serenaded the beavers as they worked. As Billy swam through the cool water, he felt incredible. The pristine wilderness seemed especially beautiful now. The first part of his dream was complete and he could now build his lodge in peace. As far as he could see there was forest and hills. No humans could be found for miles around. No Farmers like Ed to fight with. Suddenly, an idea came to Billy and he announced out loud, "I'm going to call this place Possibility Pond. The name will remind us that often what we think is impossible is really possible, if we believe in a dream and act on it." Billy took time to enjoy what he had done and give thanks. He felt comforted knowing that dreams really can come true. Gratitude is a necessary adventure ingredient. Billy turned and looked at Chewie with grateful eyes. Without her belief and support, his dream would never have come true.

~ The End...of the beginning ~

LEARNING COMPANION 21

Conversation Points: Powerful Tools

Billy's story illustrates a basic mental law. The thoughts and goals you believe in will appear in your experience. What you place in your subconscious mind acts according to this law and works with the universe to manifest your reality. If you think you can't do something, the universe will respond and work to ensure that you don't. You must control your Egor. If you believe you can do something, then you will do it sooner or later. Billy has used some powerful tools to reinforce his Major Definite Purpose in his subconscious. Let's review them:

1. **Transmutation:** Billy constantly responded to adversity by converting his experience into a positive learning event. This is also referred to as reframing. The physical analogy would be changing lead into gold.

2. **EndPoint Visualization:** He had a clear picture of what he wanted to accomplish and he reviewed this vision constantly, especially before going to sleep and when waking up.

3. **Redefine the Challenge:** Unlike the flies that continually hit a window trying to escape from their situation, Billy came up with novel solutions to meet his need for a new home. By thinking outside of the box on many occasions and doing things that had never been tried before, or things that no one had yet done, he was able to achieve his goal.

4. **Positive Mental Attitude:** Billy continually battled Egor to keep himself positive and free of doubt and fear. He watched his language and tried to, no, **did** what he needed to do to reach his goal. Billy eliminated the word **try** from his vocabulary, a word that acknowledges failure from the start.

5. **Mastermind Alliance:** Billy established a strong Mastermind Alliance during his journey, **starting with the necessary belief in himself,** overcoming Egor, and then adding Chewie, Elder and even Willy.

6. **Gratitude Complex**: Billy was constantly thankful for the ideas and the individuals who helped him on his path. Often, it was this Gratitude Complex that defeated the voice of doubt and fear, Egor!

7. **Keep Moving Forward:** Billy took each step one day at a time. He stayed present to his environment, remained focused on his vision, and looked for clues along his journey.

Draw your Own Icons

Create icons to reinforce the concept of a Major Definite Purpose in your subconscious. For example an icon for Transmutation could be a gold fishing weight pendant hanging on a fishing line (lead to gold).

A transmutation can be a written one as well. As an example: There will always be difficulties, and they will always come with a gift. Be alert, watch for them and take action. This could be seen as a transmutation of Napoleon Hill's principle, "Every adversity, every failure, every heartache, carries with it the seed of an equal or greater benefit." Creating transmutations changes the form that information comes in, into something condensed, or something that makes sense to you. This is wonderful for fostering good memory and understanding.

• Create icons for the first seven Powerful Tools:

Draw a Gratitude Icon

Another example is #6, the Gratitude Complex. Consider an icon of you as a stick person bowing to the people you are grateful to, represented as a group of stick people. It's OK to weave in a little humour if it helps you remember. Creating Icons is also a productivity tool when used in mind mapping, as it embodies the idea that a picture is worth a thousand words. It increases the opportunity for new or related ideas that connect to or emerge from others.

8. **Ask at the Risk of Receiving**: Billy asked for help from Chewie; she responded by saying, "Yes!" If Billy had not asked, he may have avoided hearing a No, but would not have had the opportunity to receive a Yes.

9. **Suspension of Judgment**: When Billy did not judge Willy, he was able to relax in the presence of the hairy spider and receive pivotal advice.

10. **Watch your language**: Your words create your reality. You become your language. Billy fought a battle to keep his language positive and clear. As Yoda says in *Star Wars*, "There is no try, only do."

11. **Clarify the communication**: Billy asked Willy to point him in the direction of water several times. He then repeated the directions to make sure that he had correctly heard and understood them. George Bernard Shaw said, "The single biggest problem in communication is the illusion that it has taken place." By checking with Willy numerous times about the direction, and repeating them back, Billy could be confident he heard clearly what Willy meant.

12. **Going the extra mile**: Billy helped Elder and continued to be concerned about those around him and those on his quest. He practiced **Random Acts of Kindness**, which eventually helped him with his own quest.

13. **Don't take criticism personally**: Billy pushed past all the laughing and doubts of his fellow beavers time and time again. If he had reacted, he would have been giving the control of his vision to others and he might not have achieved his goal.

14. **Everything is exactly as it should be**: When adversities popped up for Billy, he identified their benefit and moved beyond them to continue to focus on his dream, instead of falling into questioning, blame, and guilt.

15. **Identify postage stamps of opportunity**: Several times in the story Billy recognized the moments when he must act quickly to change the course of his life and to reach his goal or the opportunity would pass.

16. **Respect the advice of your elders**: By valuing Elder's life experience and listening to the ideas he had to share, Billy benefitted greatly and eventually succeeded in achieving his MDP.

17. **Having the proper motivation**: Billy did not use hate and revenge as a motivator, even though he certainly could have hated farmer Ed, or carried a grudge against the beavers that laughed at him.

Knowledge Nugget!

Icons are so important.

If you start a business, or create a service, your logo is especially critical. Sandy and I love the logo we created for our seminars. We like to share it as it tells an all-important story. In the north, with the seemingly infinite stretches of white, inukshuks are used to guide people, which is illustrated by our logo.

Our Personal Greatness Seminar teaches people how to set a vision (curved arch) or MDP, and how important a Mastermind Alliance is (the two figures) to become a success (remember, you need to take other with you on your journey). By incorporating these elements into our logo, we felt it illustrated some of the principles taught in our seminar.

- Draw icons for Powerful Tools 8-17:

Knowledge Nugget!

Spend Your Life Currency With Care

As a result of accomplishing an amazing goal, Billy will realize that the most precious thing he has is his time, and not to waste a minute. Carl Sandburg said, "Time is the most valuable coin in your life." Be careful how you spend it. Our lives are bounded by birth and death, and in between is everything you desire to achieve. Billy has experienced and accomplished much through his ambitious goal.

Possibility Pond

18. **Getting even is wasteful.** Carrying a grudge gives you a negative mental attitude that causes your mind to work poorly. It is like throwing iron filings into a machine. Keep in mind that the universe needs no help dealing out consequences. If you take action to get even with someone, then remember the saying, "What goes around, comes around." If you give out love then it will come back to you. If you give out hate then it will come back to you. Babylonian King Hammurabi (c.1790 BC) decreed, "An eye for an eye, a tooth for a tooth". Centuries later Ghandi responded with, "It will make the whole world blind and toothless." Forgiveness will be a positive life changing idea for you to adopt.

19. **Watch your words and labels**: Billy decided to name his lodge Possibility Pond as a reminder that what he think is impossible is actually possible. In his quest, he repeated Impossible Creek many times as he shared his dream and identified the stream. Retelling the Impossible Creek story would be a poor EPV and become self-defeating if he let *impossible* sink into his subconscious.

20. **Billy developed excellent habits**: The habits we develop are taken up by the sub-conscious mind and performed as if we are on automatic pilot. Billy learned to control his mind and by the end of the story; this ability became a habit. When he creates another MDP in the future and pursues it, his task will be much easier. Aristotle lectured on the power of habits, "Excellence is not an act, but a habit." You are where you are, and what you are because of your established habits of thoughts and deeds. James Clear's best-selling book, *Atomic Habits* is a must read for anyone wishing to complete a challenging MDP. Develop good habits using the principles in this book

21. **Assume responsibility for your own destiny**: There is no hint of blame on Billy's part when things go wrong. Although he worked closely with his Mastermind Alliance, he practiced the affirmation, "If it is to be, then it is up to me." Billy was 100% responsible for what he experienced. When faced with a seemingly impossible task, he persevered and came up with the solution.

Learning Points: Continue Learning

Examine books, magazines and real-life stories to identify Success Principles and see how they are applied. Principles Billy used are being applied by people every day. Learn from others who live their success.

Enjoy the life you love, NOW!

Freedom of Self-Expression

A summary benefit for Billy is that he experienced the freedom to be and express himself, the freedom to believe what he liked, the freedom to imagine, and the freedom of his emotions and character. These are all huge benefits.

• Draw icons for Power Tools 18-21.

Pass a Compliment Along When You Hear One

A powerful habit worth developing (#20) is to compliment others, and to pass-on compliments you hear about others. When a person shares their positive experience of another person, rather than leaving it as a nice story, seek out the person who was mentioned and share the compliment. You will see how powerful it is and how this simple act can build up another person. Be alert for opportunities to directly compliment others. For example, if you have a fine meal at a restaurant, seek out the chef and let them know how wonderful it was. If the service was great, let your server know. Not only do you spread goodwill and gratitude, you benefit with a sense of wellbeing as well. This powerful act can change cultures, such as teams, corporations, neighbourhoods and families.

APPENDIX

Believe

Luke McMaster

Put that picture in your mind
Reach up for the sky
Never lose your faith
'Cause tomorrow's a brand new day

Chorus:
When you believe
That it's possible
You will achieve it
You're unstoppable
You can reach up to the stars
Shining down on you
No matter what the distance
You will make it through
When you believe

Should you ever feel afraid
Just breathe in then exhale
Keep your goal in sight
Nothing comes without a fight

(Chorus)

There's a picture in your mind
Of the life you want to live
There's no such thing as try
Give all you've got to give

(Chorus)

Scan the QR code with your mobile device camera,
or use this link to hear the song: Believe
tinyurl.com/believe-song

20 Success Principles: Definitions and Tips for Remembering

Here is a summary of the 17 Success Principles identified by Napoleon Hill, plus 3 additional principles I believe enhance success. I have found the list to be useful when analyzing whether someone is appropriate for certain tasks. It is also useful for evaluating the progress of your Mastermind Alliance. Also, the principles can be helpful in the 9/11 exercise, where you list 9 of your positive attributes, and 11 reasons why you will be successful in most endeavours. The principles are listed in a logical order, with tips to help you remember them by number.

1. **A Major Definite Purpose (MDP)**: Something significant yet to do. This is often a challenge for elderly people. It is also the number 1 challenge for most of us. It requires singleness of purpose.

2. **A Mastermind Alliance (MMA)**: No one person can be a success without taking others with them. You need to bring at least one more person with you to achieve your goals. Think two or more.

3. **Faith (F!)**: Belief that your MDP will happen. This will give you courage when the going gets tough. Having faith will help you stay positive on your journey. For number 3 think, Trinity, to remember this important attribute.

4. **Go the Extra Mile (GEM)**: Providing a service to others when none is expected. This idea often takes you into new realms that provide ideas for your journey. It can help identify MMA members. Think, "4-minute mile" as your memory prompt.

5. **Personal Initiative (PI)** : You can start projects on your own by reaching out. An example would be walking up to a stranger, introducing yourself and shaking their hand (five fingers).

6. **Pleasing Personality (PP)**: I love chocolate. Hotel 6 used to put a chocolate on the pillow, a pleasing gesture.

7. **Positive Mental Attitude (PMA)**: The mind works better with positivity. A medical person shared with me, "I do not have the luxury of even one negative thought." A positive attitude makes a difference. Think of dice, rolling a lucky 7 to win.

8. **Enthusiasm (E!)**: This represents an intense and eager enjoyment or interest. Turn 8 on its side and you get an infinity symbol ∞ , the ethos of enthusiasm.

9. **Self-Discipline (SD)**: William Johnsen said, "If it is to be it is up to me." This is a great habit. It requires you to keep your eye on the ball. In yoga, the tree pose requires discipline by standing on one leg. In this pose your body is shaped like a 9.

10. **Accurate Thinking (AT)**: Requires you to be skeptical of self, others and associated information. Place the 1 over the 0 vertically and you have the cross-hairs of a scope, which allows you to focus accurately: ϕ

11. **Controlled Attention (CA)**: You do not want to be a wandering generality. Once you have the word attention, the controlled portion follows. Two ones together (11) look like two people standing at attention.

12. **Teamwork (T!)**: Team is an acronym for **T**ogether **E**ach **A**chieves **M**ore. "1, 2, let's go!" is the team call to action.

13. **Learning From Adversity and Defeat (LFAD)**. Einstein said, "In the middle of difficulty lies opportunity." Look for the opportunity as soon as the difficulty is encountered. Your ability to do this is your Adversity Quotient (AQ). Rather than unlucky 13, consider it to be opportunity knocking.

14. **Creative Thinking (CT)**: I always think that this requires you to look around for ideas. I recall standing on a lookout, attempting to figure out where to go. I pictured a 1 on the left and a 4 touching it on the right, creating a symbolic viewing tower. (Use your imagination; it's called creative thinking…right?)

15. **Budget Time and Money (BTM)**: Don't waste energy and resources, choose how to use them. Place the 1 over the 5 and you have a dollar sign ($). Time and money will follow once you remember the dollar sign.

16. **Health (H!)**: Eat well. Eat mostly live food that has life force in it. Stay away from processed food and sugar. That is certainly a desirable goal for life. Think, "Sweet 16!" an age when one is healthy and vibrant.

17. **Cosmic Habit Force (CHF)**: Establishing good habits is essential. The word cosmic relates to things like the earth going around the sun once a year. *Atomic Habits* by James Clear is an essential read. I have created a habit of exercising for 2

hours every day. Dynamic Yogic Breathing for 45 minutes, sun salutations and other yoga poses, plus cardio and weights. Think of a memory mnemonic for yourself. To remember that the 17th principle is Cosmic, I recall that I took a university astronomy course when I was 17. What is your memory key?

18. **Determination (D!)**: Winston Churchill in a famous speech said, "Never, never, never … never give up." This one idea can be compared to a dog with a bone that won't let go. It has carried me to my goal when it seemed that it was impossible. Repeat to yourself, "Just keep doing it!" Or to quote Dory, Nemo's friend in the movie *Finding Dory*, "Keep swimming!" An image for determination is: 1 for single mindedness and 8 on its side as the symbol for infinite firmness of purpose: 1 ∞

19. **Persistence (P!)**: Continuing a course of action or opinion despite difficulty or opposition. In moving to your MDP, you are likely going to encounter adversity. View the adversity as opportunity to learn or find another path to your goal. To remember, flip the 9 to a "P" and you have I.P. for, "I Persist!"

> *Nothing in the world can take the place of persistence. Talent will not; nothing is more common than unsuccessful men with talent. Genius will not; unrewarded genius is almost a proverb. Education will not; the world is full of educated derelicts. Persistence and determination alone are omnipotent.* -- Calvin Coolidge.

20. **Adaptability to Change (A2C)**: It is said that change is the one constant in this life. Many people lament changing weather and must think that there is a thermostat in the sky that can adjust it. We waste valuable time trying to change what we cannot. Accept what is and live your life to the fullest. Keep your eyes open for opportunity. To remember 20, think Version 2.0, adapting to change.

How to Memorize the 20 Success Principles

You can use Success Principles in many situations. For example, writing a reference letter, I use the principles to help me decide what to say on behalf of the person.

Repeating the list is also an effective mind conditioner. As you remember each of the 20 Success Principles, count from 1 to 20 and form a mental image for each principle. This creates a link to the material for easy and thorough recall. Here is a quick list to review with suggested memory cues. Feel free to come up with memory cues that work for you:

1. **Major Definite Purpose (MDP)**: Your #1 challenge
2. **Mastermind Alliance (MMA)**: 2 or more people
3. **Faith (F!)**: Trinity (3)
4. **Go the Extra Mile (GEM)**: 4-minute mile
5. **Personal Initiative (PI)**: 5 fingers to shake hands
6. **Pleasing Personality (PP)**: Hotel 6 chocolate
7. **Positive Mental Attitude (PMA)**: Roll 7 to win!
8. **Enthusiasm (E!)**: Infinity symbol ∞
9. **Self-Discipline (SD)**: Stand on 1 leg, the 9 pose
10. **Accurate Thinking (AT)**: $1+0 = \phi$
11. **Controlled Attention (CA)**: Two at attention
12. **Teamwork (T!)**: 1, 2, let's go! Team call to action
13. **Learning from Adversity and Defeat (LFAD)** Lucky 13 is opportunity knocking
14. **Creative Thinking (CT)**: 1 left, 4 right = tower
15. **Budget Time and Money (BTM)**: 1 over 5 = $
16. **Health (H!)**: Sweet 16!
17. **Cosmic Habit Force (CHF)**: Power at age 17
18. **Determination (D!)**: $1+\infty$ = single-minded to infinity
19. **Persistence (P!)** : $1+9 = I+P = I$ Persist
20. **Adaptability to Change (A2C)**: Version 2.0

Use the Success Principle Checklist/Log on the last page to track your use of the 20 principles.

Contact the author to share your memory aids. His email is on the copyright page.

Template: Your Major Definite Purpose (MDP)

A. Define Your Major Definite Purpose

What follows is a template, based on the works of Napoleon Hill, to guide you in the development of your Major Definite Purpose (MDP). A real-life example is provided to illustrate how these steps can be put into action. Use the present tense in your statements, as if the goal has already been accomplished. State your goal clearly, with a clear plan for its achievement.

The Template

1. **MDP**: Write a clear statement of your goal.

Ideally it is a concise phrase (10 words or less) that can be remembered and easily repeated before bed and in the morning. The following exercise will help you get a clear EndPoint Vision (EPV) of your MDP.

   a. **Knowledge**: List the knowledge you need to acquire. Write down the motive for acquiring that knowledge. Keep in mind that some of the knowledge you lack can be made up by a careful choice of people in your Mastermind Alliance, or by hiring help. You don't have to know it all; you do need to know where to find it. Some people use extensive preparation as a way of procrastinating. In this case, valuable advice is, Just Do It! In starting We Care Health Services, we did not have all the expertise. We learned as we went along.

   b. **Action**: Specify the kind of action you will take while working toward a goal. Being clear about what you are doing while pursuing your MDP is important; it will sustain you along the way. Also, list the kind of work that achieving the goal will lead you to perform. This will help you maintain a clear vision of where you are going. Specify your motives for your actions and for your goal. My book *EndPoint Vision and Beyond* contains a template similar to the one on the next page.

   c. **Earnings**: Consider how much you wish to earn while pursuing your MDP and once you have achieved it. Also list the motives connected to this money, and how you intend to use it. Consider donating to good causes.

   d. **Personality**: State the personality that you wish to bring into your MDP. For example, if your MDP is to be in a loving relationship, consider the qualities that you will bring to that relationship such as mutual respect, humour, commitment and loyalty.

   e. **Travel**: If travel is part of your MDP, consider where it might take you. Make a clear statement about the places you wish to go and your motives for this desire.

   f. **Skills**: Write down the skills that you need to acquire, through formal learning or from someone/something else, along with your motives for acquiring these skills. Caution: One can suffer from paralysis by analysis by spending too much time in learning mode vs. action mode. Socrates said, "For the things we need to do, but don't know how, we learn by doing." For things you cannot learn yourself, find someone who already has the knowledge. They might become a part of your Mastermind Alliance (MMA).

   g. **Motives**: List all the motives that you can think of for accomplishing your goal. This helps you create the passion you will need for action and to program your MDP into your subconscious.

2. **Benefits**: List the benefits that you will receive as a result of accomplishing your MDP.

3. **Commitment**: Sign a statement as a contract between you and Egor, your sub-conscious mind. For example, Jim Carrey, the actor wrote himself a check for a million dollars. This was the contract he made with himself to keep focused on his goal to become a star.

4. **Repeat Daily**: Read your MDP aloud at least two times daily. The best times to do this are when you get up in the morning and before you go to sleep. When you sleep, that great computer, your subconscious, can work on ways to achieve your goal. Complete the 9/11 practice described in the Learning Companion for chapter 4 and then repeat it daily for 91 days to anchor it into your psyche.

B. Accomplish Your MDP

1. **Plan**: Write a clear plan for achieving your Major Definite Purpose (MDP). Include the following:

   - **Time** needed to achieve your MDP or to get it to a point where it is self-sustaining. For example, if you form a company, it may be managed by others.

   - **Divide and Conquer** your MDP into units of effort, with minor goals, action plans and time frames for each. My book *EndPoint Vision and Beyond,* describes these as Critical Events on your path, that are required for success.

   - **Decide** what you intend to give, or give up, to achieve your MDP. You never get something for nothing. What can you give back to make a difference in the world? For example, Vic Lindal and I wrote *Radical Coaching: Strategies for Winning.* We donated copies to a coach in Zimbabwe for use as a training manual in a volleyball camp. His MDP is helping youth out of poverty and preparing a team to qualify for the Olympics.

   - **Allow for flexibility**. Your Mastermind Alliance and the universe will throw opportunities your way that you never expected. Trust infinite intelligence to deliver needed ideas.

2. **Confidentiality**: When sharing any of your ideas and plans for your Major Definite Purpose, consider using selective confidentiality. Those who are not interested in or are not committed to your dream can dissipate your power for accomplishment. They may be friends and family who feel protective and want you to avoid taking risks. Others may not want you to succeed because they are envious or jealous, and can consciously or unconsciously sabotage your success.

   Continually work to keep your mind on what you desire, and off what you don't want. It is a challenge when people bring up negative scenarios that challenge your dream, so avoid them. Napoleon Hill advises, "Do not plant seeds on rocky ground." So be aware of challenges. There are useful checklists. I use the five Ps to evaluate a business opportunity: Product, Price, Promotion, Place and People. For example, when I look at a start-up, Place is key. Has the entrepreneur chosen a business location that will support success or doom their business before they start? Be careful!

Your MMA will be valuable in assessing reality.

MAJOR DEFINITE PURPOSE (MDP) TEMPLATE

1. Major Definite Purpose:

a. Knowledge needed:

b. Action to take:

c. Earning goal:

d. Preferred personality:

e. Travel:

f. Skills:

g. Motives:

2. Benefits:

3. Contract with myself:

Date:

Signature:

Applying Goal Setting to a Major Definite Purpose

In the following section I share my personal experience and the experience of others, to illustrate how Success Principles can be applied to your life and to the process of setting and achieving your MDP.

My Major Definite Purpose (MDP) is to bring Success Principles to the Canadian population. I am doing this by partnering with a corporation that is adopting this material into their business plan and work culture, to enhance its impact on their clients, employees and leadership team.

Writing about the past and future in the present tense allows me to live my MDP in the present, so I enjoy the feelings of success as if my goal is achieved.

The following details develop, refine and maintain a clear path for my Major Definite Purpose (MDP):

1. *Knowledge I am acquiring*:
   a) I am off to a great start. I am fortunate to be trained in Napoleon Hill's Success Principles, which we apply with remarkable success to our company. We Care Health Services grows to 64 franchises. Using the *Possibility Pond* book is instrumental to our success.
   b) While seeking ways to run positive and cooperative franchises, I discover that these principles work extremely well in the business world. I also introduce my family to them with positive results. Sharing these principles with my son Luke, who is a member of the award winning musical duo McMaster and James, enables him to develop a plan for signing with a major music label. My son Rob applies the principles to achieve designation as a forensic psychiatrist.
   c) I continue to hone my writing skills. I work with Reciprocity Publishing to publish my first two books: *EndPoint Vision and Beyond* and *Radical Coaching*. I publish my third book, *Possibility Pond*, which applies my knowledge of the Success Principles.

2. *My EndPoint Vision:*
   a) *Possibility Pond* inspires a series of smaller books that highlight each of the Success Principles in more detail. They focus on children as the primary though not exclusive audience. I use a variety of formats to deliver the material and advertise the seminars.

3. My motive for doing this is my love of making a difference in the world by helping individuals and families live the best life they can. This spurs me on. It is fulfilling to receive recognition from many individuals and families for my positive contribution to their journey. I am also motived by a desire for self-expression.

4. *Kind of work I am doing:*
   a) I am delivering Success Principles 101 courses and training instructors. I am giving talks at conferences and to a variety of community clubs. I am giving interviews on the value of the principles in *Possibility Pond* and *EndPoint Vision and Beyond*. *Possibility Pond* is being used for corporate training as the characters are animals that allow readers to learn key principles and avoid judgment and finger pointing at people.
   b) I am making this material available on the Internet as well as in hard copy books. I am writing books for children, adults and corporations that teach Success Principles and concepts such as those inspired by Don Miguel Ruiz's best seller, *The Four Agreements*.
   c) My motive is recognition from others for having made a difference in their lives and in the world, and for the gift of self-expression. I love being free in body, mind and more. Simply stated, I love to be my own boss. Also, it is a labor of love to write, learn, share, and teach.
   d) A mirror can shine light into dark places. I work to shine Success Principles into the lives of people who need them and can use them to achieve their desired win.

5. *Personality I am cultivating:*
   a) I am a motivator and a mentor. I am fortunate to have been successful academically, in business, and in relationships. After people work with me, they have the courage to take risks and to pursue their dreams. I am an exciting, knowledgeable and caring person. People want to be around me. I absolutely cherish the recognition that this brings to me.
   b) My life embodies the following statement, "If I can be of assistance to you, do not hesitate

to ask." I first heard this statement from Viktor Frankl, the author of *Man's Search for Meaning*, during a franchise training session. I had the opportunity to speak with him after a franchisee asked me where I acquired some of my ideas. I initiated a call to express my gratitude for his inspiration. My assistant was able to locate Viktor Frankl in Vienna and get him on the speaker phone. We had a conversation in the presence of the conference participants, during which I was able to tell him that he was making a difference to 4500 people in our corporation. It was during this conversation that he made his offer of assistance, and I have adopted his attitude ever since.

Several months later he died. I am so grateful for applying the wisdom, "Do it when you think of it," as it opened an opportunity that would have been forever closed by his passing. So often we put things off and then it is too late, or we waste time reconsidering the action over and over, also known as procrastination. Viktor Frankl also gave me another term for Major Definite Purpose, which was, "Something significant yet to do."

6. *Wish to Earn:*

- I write myself a cheque for $50,000, that is cashable in three years. From my desire to give back to the world, I donate expertise and financial support. To that end, I am setting up seminars where families and corporations can learn Success Principles and the practice of being in a successful Mastermind Alliance.

7. *Places I wish to visit each year:*

- I visit places such as the spiritual canyons and buttes in New Mexico, the ancient Sitka spruce trees on Vancouver Island, Thailand, the ruins in Peru, further yoga training in Rishikish India. My motivation is closely tied to learning about life after death. I am as whole a person as possible.

8. *Skills, Arts, Crafts, Sciences needed:*

- I am continually developing my writing, speaking and communication skills. My Toastmasters public speaking and leadership club is a great vehicle to carry me toward this goal. Self-expression and recognition are paramount motivators for me. External recognition is important, as is the internal recognition I have of myself..

9. *General motives:*

- I desire to make a difference in the world and to strive for excellence in everything I do. The joy of transforming people's lives for the better is an awesome experience.

10. *Five Year Plan:*

- *Possibility Pond* book is widely distributed.
- I am giving my course, Success Principles 101, and the companion instructor course, every year at major centres in Canada.
- A feature story about the book is written in a prominent magazine.
- I am on Canada AM promoting books and seminars.
- I distribute the book *Possibility Pond* widely.
- I make appearances on talk shows and podcasts.

The first step is to get a publisher…Done!

The next step is to get a major corporate backer for *Possibility Pond*.

To achieve my goal, I am investing my most precious commodity: time, my life currency. I am dedicating a portion of my personal funds and savings to see that this goal is reached.

We all need to understand: Time is our Life Currency; we need to be vigilant in how we spend it.

A note on simplicity:

If you can't explain it simply, you probably do not understand it well enough. Our granddaughter Marlowe, when 10 years old, said to my wife and I, "You are loving and you adventureize." This describes our Major Definite Purpose. When you travel, at all times be aware of making the world a loving and better place.

An expanded explanation of "adventureize" is included at the end of this book. It is especially good advice for seniors.

Success Stories

Many of the principles in this book have been applied by famous people such as Henry Ford (a pioneer in streamlining the automobile assembly line) and Thomas Edison (one of the most famous inventors). Where does that leave ordinary people like you and me? Your MDP may look different, as we each define success differently. The point is that by applying the principles in this book, you too can be your own version of success. Financial success and fame are two possibilities; there are so many more. You may wish to find a loving relationship, support the endeavours of your children, be the best volunteer, or master a skill. The sky is the limit.

A. An Immigrant's Story

Can ordinary people achieve success? Yes! The following story illustrates this point effectively. It is about Sue Ismiel, a young Syrian girl who moved to Australia with her family. At the age of 15, she dropped out of school and took a job as a doctor's receptionist. Today, she is an inventor and the creator of a company called NADS, which grosses over $40 million AUD in business a year. Here is her story:

First the adversity: one of her three daughters, Natalie, at the age of 6, was self-conscious about the dark hair on her arms. She also had sensitive skin, which made the usual methods of hair removal a problem. Sue can summarize her Major Definite Purpose in 10 easy to remember words, "Remove unwanted hair from the most sensitive skin, without irritation." A mother's love for her child became the prime motivating factor, and is certainly one of the strongest from the list of motivators. At the time, Sue was a hospital clerical worker with no chemistry background, and there were already many multinational corporations who specialized in removing unwanted hair.

At this point in the story, stop yourself and estimate Sue's chances for success, on a scale of 0 to 100. Then review the definition of genius on page 67, and again estimate her chances for success. A big change!

Now we'll continue with the story. With her clear goal, Sue used her instincts, her kitchen stove and pantry as her chemistry laboratory. She also believed that she could invent something. Her whole family helped test her experimental concoctions. Her husband Sam, a member of her Mastermind Alliance, often couldn't wear shorts because of the spot marks from Sue's hair removal trials. Was her desire strong and was it lodged in her subconscious, that great bio computer?

Sue spoke about her daughter's hair problem, "Poor baby. It became like an obsession with me. I really wanted something for her." After a year of experimenting, and conducting trials on her family, Ismiel came up with a solution. The right mixture of honey, vinegar, molasses, water and lemon juice made up the ingredients of her Green Goo that worked successfully and avoided the hot torture of waxing. Today, NADS is the best-selling depilatory in the USA.

Sue Ismiel's advice?

"There is always a way. 'Never take no for an answer' is the greatest trait of every successful individual."

"I had to block the outside world to protect myself from all the negatives inundating me."

I encourage you to find your own success stories that inspire you to follow your own vision and passion. May you achieve your dreams!

B. An Artist's Story

The search for the right artist became a real adventure, much like Billy Beaver's challenge to find a new home for his colony. Many ideas in the story assisted me greatly and provided a good template for the search.

I have always agreed with the statement that "A picture is worth a thousand words." Further to that belief, a picture with accompanying words is worth much more to our understanding and remembering of a story than pictures on their own.

Therefore it was imperative that I find great illustrations to accompany the story of Billy Beaver.

When I began work on the book I did some rough sketches of how I imagined Possibility Pond and Happy Valley might look. This guided my writing in a positive way. As the story unfolded, I wanted to teach the ideas contained in the story and felt that my graphics were too primitive to add much to the presentation. After interviewing many young artists and their sample sketches, I chose one to create the landscapes and characters to accompany the story. I then taught the course with those graphics. They were good illustrations but they did not bring the story to life in the way I envisioned. I never lost the belief that I would eventually find that right artist and so my search continued. Along the journey, I interviewed artists who used computer technology as well as those who did hand sketches, but with no meaningful success.

Many years later, I attended a drawing course taught by Mr. Albert Casson, a relation to A.J. Casson one of the members of the famous Canadian Group of Seven. Casson's class was a breath taking and inspiring adventure. Given the conviction of my belief that I would find a great artist at some point, I felt sure I had finally found them. Armed with the ideas which are embedded in the story: how to achieve your EndPoint Vision, Ask at the risk of receiving, Keep Moving Forward (KMF), and Whatever the mind can conceive and believe, then it is possible to achieve it, I took a chance and somewhat nervously approached Albert to asked him if he would consider illustrating the story.

I provided Albert with the version of the story and the illustrations that I had been using while teaching. He read the story and said enthusiastically he wanted to be part of a journey that could help people be successful in whatever they undertook. Albert is a well-known wildlife, portrait and landscape artist and he connected to the story in a deep and meaningful way. He identified closely with the character Elder and embraced the principles immediately. Elder was instrumental in helping the group's success at key times. I had found my Elder and knew without a doubt Billy and his community would be brought to life in the way I had envisioned when I began this journey.

C. The Mastermind Alliance (MMA)

What follows are some of my personal experiences illustrating one of the most critical principles of success, the Mastermind Alliance (MMA). I offer examples of how the practice of this principle has impacted my life and my family in unimaginably positive ways. My wife and I have taught many seminars based on *Possibility Pond*. This joint knowledge of Success Principles has created a strong foundation for our relationship and made our lives wonderful. This concept has deeply impacted our relationship with my sons, and has contributed to deepening our relationships with them and their families.

Establishing a family MMA

This first example illustrates how an alliance was formed with the four sons. Our vision is that by using our MMA knowledge, we can assist them to strengthen their bonds, allowing them to be mutually supportive of each other in work and play, and with each of their respective families and of course, with my wife and I. Hence we formed an informal MMA with them, sharing experiences, food, conversation and lots of laughs.

Ten years ago, my wife asked me what I wanted for my birthday. I immediately replied that I wanted to spend four days with my sons and my brother, Jim. In collaboration with the youngest son, Robert, she was able to pull it off. A cottage was rented and the six of us had a marvelous four days, trying our hand at Pickleball, sharing meals, conversation and laughs. We like variety, and in the years that followed, we pursued other pleasurable activities including golf, boating, and fishing. This MMA gathering is now in its tenth year and shows no signs of stopping.

An unexpected and important by-product of our first weekend together was the creation of a private social media thread that allows us to maintain contact throughout the year and coordinate the annual gathering with ease. We are now in touch almost daily sharing ideas about living a life we love, exchanging thoughts, and encouraging and supporting each other.

It also allows us to schedule gatherings at other times of the year for a meal, a weekend together or a ping-pong tournament at Christmas. This Mastermind Alliance opened the door to a stronger, more supportive family, which trickles down to our grandchildren, who benefit from examples of how to live a life they love, from their parents and grandparents.

For the first year, my wife organized the weekend. Since then, Robert has stepped up to help find the retreat location each year, organized food and suggested activities for the group to consider. The culinary creations improve every year and we have all learned new dishes to share with each other.

We created a unique logo using MMW as an acronym for McMaster Men's Weekend. This logo also serves to remind us that a **Master Mind Wins**. Each year my wife has caps and shirts made that feature the logo. Some of the grandchildren love this merchandise and are often seen wearing it throughout the year. It has the wonderful effect of enhancing the MMW event within the family and focusing them on the MMA concept. They are anxious to join this annual event. Additionally, some of our sons' friends like the MMW 'merch' and want to purchase items.

Forming an MMA with our grandchildren

What about our grandchildren who want to join the MMW? We decided to introduce an off-shoot of the gathering so they could build their own events and memories. We created an MMA with them complete with a new agenda. This new gathering was created at their suggestion, around two powerful trilogies, *The Hobbit* and *The Lord of the Rings*, movies based on Tolkien's books. Our grandsons love them and the life messages they express. These movies encapsulate many Success Principles and viewing them inspires our time together. It is an epic adventure that motivates us to strike out on adventures together.

The definition for an adventure is "an unusual and exciting or daring experience". The term 'adventurizing' describes this initiative perfectly. The weekend has become an adventure we undertake together, watching all six movies, preparing meals together and having experiences that enhance the scenes we watch unfold in the movies. Each movie lasts 3 hours. Following each one, we take turns describing what we liked, what we learned and the success concepts embedded in the stories. To break up the day we include outdoor activities that parallel some of the adventures we are watching. In the movie, the fellowship travels down a river with forests on both banks. We have one such river nearby and we incorporate a long hike followed by an immersion in the river to mimic a little of the adventure we are watching.

As Einstein says, "You are only limited by your imagination." So with the grandsons, my wife Sandy and I created the name, Master Mind Fellowship (MMF). This MMF name directly connects us to the adventures in the movies, *Fellowship of the Ring* It is another way to express a Mastermind Alliance.

After our fourth MMF year, two of the boys will be going to University and we will likely end up changing some of the parameters of the gathering. Change is constant and expected, creating the possibility of new challenges. However, we have a strong MMF and they have a strong desire for the fellowship to continue.

Here is a glimpse of a meal activity which we enjoyed, to give you a sense of how we introduce adventure. In the Hobbit, the dwarves have a feast, so we decided a dwarf feast would be part of the weekend. This included using their hands and only a knife during the meal, just like the dwarves. When asked what they wanted as part of the menu, one of the grandsons took an adventurous step and replied, "I would like to try rabbit." This choice was inspired by a scene in one of the movies when coneys (rabbits) were caught by the creature Gollum and prepared by Samwise. Sandy cooked this meal for the MMF. Initially they were hesitant to try it. We encouraged them to get out of the "same ole' same ole' box," to be like the dwarves and try a new adventure. Something surprising happened. At first they nibbled, and then liking what they tasted, proceeded to load their plates with the rabbit attempting to get their full share.

When we met with their parents afterwards, the MMF jumped out of the van, telling their parents it was the best time ever and could they eat with knives at home. Mom and Dad were delighted however, they would not be allowing them to eat only with knives at home.

The success principle concepts of MDP (Major Definite Purpose), MMA (Mastermind Alliance), our MMF (Mastermind Fellowship) and the other Success Principles, have helped us build closeness with our family and within our relationship that we cherish. For all of you parents, grandparents and adventurers, I encourage you to embrace these powerful principles and create your own wonderful adventures.

A spinoff that I love is that all seven of our grandchildren want the ideas of the MMF to pervade our family thinking. You cannot be a success unless you have the language of success and we have all been inoculated with the language of success found in Billy's *Possibility Pond* story. The MMF concept has made it easier for us to bond with the grand kids, something we are truly grateful for.

The Power of ICONS.

We are a picture processing species. Though text may be necessary for understanding; a picture can be worth a thousand words, and a picture with text can be worth ten times that much. If I say, "Garbage can," you don't immediately see the words. It's the image of a garbage can that comes to mind.

We discussed the use of Icons to compress information, and to aid memory and speed of communication. Amazing benefits! It is so powerful an idea that icons are used as logos to readily identify a company or organization. The McMaster Men Weekend logo mentioned above is immediately recognizable to the members of our family MMA. It conjures up great memories and anticipated good times. Flip it and you have one for the McMasters Women's Weekend!

The tennis pro Roger Federer compressed his initials, creating extra style. Emojis are another great example of icons.

The Role of This Book in Life's Journey

Early research from Stanford University indicated that on average we will have 5 careers in a lifetime. It is now suggested that this number has increased to 16. Our world is changing rapidly, driven by the new technologies of the Internet, computers and smart phones. Social media and artificial intelligence (AI) software applications drastically alter our daily lives, work, and social fabric. Communication tools and technological advancements also impact the global economy. Imagine inoculating ourselves and our children with concepts that help us create the life we desire and allow us to transition through rapid change successfully. This is my goal, and the purpose of this book is to make this vision a reality. I see all families, communities and ultimately countries working together as a Mastermind Alliance (MMA).

A. Attracting the Life You Would Love to Live

It has been over 30 years since the idea for *Possibility Pond* first came into being. In 1994 I began to write a story on the application of Success Principles so readers could learn the principles in a relaxed and practical way. The result was *Possibility Pond*, which told the story of Billy Beaver and how he applied the laws of success for living the life he wanted. It also became the workbook for the Success Principles 101 seminar I taught to businesses, professionals, parents and families for 24 years. Since that time, I have been able to reflect on the lessons of Billy's story and have come to experience the workings of the Success Principles and the law of attraction in my own life. This book has had a profound effect on me. I will share my experience of how the power of the mind can impact one's life.

I am adding these personal reflections to Billy's story, to demonstrate how putting the principles into action can create a way of approaching one's life that works. The initial impetus for the book was my feeling of inspiration when I witnessed how well Success Principles worked when applied to daily living. I saw them change the lives of individuals, families and businesses for the better, and came to understand that if these principles were taught at an early age, life would hold so much more possibility. Personally, I experienced how the power of the mind can draw into my life the things I most desire, and if not vigilant, things I do not want. This convinced me that Success Principles are powerful and accessible tools for creating a wonderful life.

Following are stories of the Success Principles in action. Some stories are from my own experiences and others are those I witnessed. Napoleon Hill once said, **"Whatever the mind can conceive and believe, it is possible to achieve."** This concept will be apparent throughout this section. Awareness of your thoughts and the power of your mind can move you along the path of success.

To understand the ability to manifest (also known as the law of attraction), I believe one must become aware of those moments in your life you might be inclined to call coincidences or synchronicities. As you observe these in the form of events, experiences, interactions, relationships, and lifestyles, note them carefully and start considering whether they connect to an earlier thought or feeling. You may find it surprising just how many experiences line up with what has occurred in your mind. It may be as simple as remembering a dear friend and presto!, they show up in your life. Pay attention, for building awareness is a key skill for success. It is also worth noting that, just like anyone else, the Universe likes to be recognized. A heartfelt expression of gratitude goes a long way to bringing on more success. Dr. Joe Dispenza says, "Gratitude is the highest form of receiving."

B. The Natural World Responds to Your Thoughts

A story of owls: My earliest experiences of the power of the mind came in the form of owls. It is my understanding that First Nations People carry traditions that connect them deeply with the natural world. These teachings helped me pay attention to experiences I may have otherwise dismissed. I had an affinity for these magnificent birds and the idea of a wise old owl always held an attraction for me that left me wanting to be connected to them. They are a bird of power in many cultures, and hold a special place in human mythology. I found them fascinating. It was not long after I had this thought that my cousin brought over two owls that had died after being caught in a trap line in the Canadian North. What to do with them? I decided to learn a little taxidermy, and I was able to successfully preserve one of these beautiful birds.

What followed was a period of time in which I began receiving owls under the most unusual circumstances. In one case, the Department of Lands and Forests in Brandon, Manitoba called me. They said an owl had hit a barbed wire fence after being blinded by car headlights, and asked me if I wanted it. I readily accepted the offer and had the owl preserved by a professional taxidermist, bringing my collection up to two. At the time of the call, I asked how they ever got my name and they were unable to tell me.

At a later date, while driving to the family cottage with my elderly mother, an owl flew in front of our truck and was hit. I leapt out of the vehicle and tried to save this beautiful bird. It did not survive and I felt I could not leave such an amazing animal to decay. Back to the taxidermist I went with this beautiful bird. I now had three owls!

You'd think this would be the end of the owl story, however they continued to manifest in my life for a little longer. The owner of a restaurant near our summer cottage must have noticed the owls in our cottage during a visit and asked if I would like the owl on the wall in her restaurant. This one was mounted as if in attack mode and frightened her niece. It came to reside at the cottage and brought the collection to four!

When Sandy and I married, we invited this same person to our wedding. Although she couldn't attend, she gave us a gift certificate. I had an inkling of what the present might be and didn't jump to tell my new wife about it. On a return trip from Winnipeg I casually mentioned to her that we should probably pick up the gift as it was on our way home. Arriving in the small town, we looked for the place named on the gift certificate, and surprise!, it was a taxidermy shop. Once I convinced Sandy to go in to collect our wedding gift, even I was shocked. Not one, but two exceptionally mounted owls awaited us. One was a snowy owl like the one in the Harry Potter movies, the other a great horned owl. The collection just expanded to six. A little bizarre, don't you think? At this point my wife suggested that perhaps I could let the universe know we had plenty of owls. I did, and no owls have materialized since then. That has been over twenty years. The law of attraction is a powerful force.

These owl stories are one illustration of how the power of our thoughts can manifest what we are thinking about. My fascination with owls and my desire to have them, allowed the universe to present them to me in a variety of unusual ways. I was not bound to a time period or the way in which they might arrive in my life, which created flexibility in how they appeared. I also accepted them when they came, even if it was not convenient at the time. This latter point is critical.

When you wish for something, the universe will deliver it to you, not necessarily on your schedule. To increase your manifestation ability, accept things at the time they are offered. Again, **expect the unexpected**.

C. The Power of Success Principles to Impact a Business

In 1984 a partner and I started a home healthcare business in response to the need of our friends who were raising a young family, and now needed to care for an ill parent. Within five years, the business grew to 20 franchises, some located in large centres such as Vancouver, Calgary and Winnipeg. Wanting to celebrate the success that we were experiencing, my partner and I held a national conference in Vancouver at a beautiful location overlooking English Bay. When I stood up to address the franchisees at the opening ceremonies and looked out, instead of seeing smiling, exuberant, grateful expressions, there were 30 grim-faced people looking back at me. My heart sank. The wonderful celebration of success I had anticipated was not to be. Here was a group of gentle, care giving nurses prepared to gallop across the home healthcare plains and leave us behind, rather than having us ride with them!

The franchisees had grown up! They were no longer the fresh faced, keen entrepreneurs who looked up to us for knowledge and guidance. They had moved on into what parents would recognize as the rebellious teenage years. Initially, knowing nothing about the business, they were receptive to paying the franchise fee and ongoing royalties in order to learn and have support as they built their business. Over time, transitioning to the adolescent stage, the franchisees now looked at us as the parents who knew nothing. The concept of paying a fee for the brand name, business system and ongoing support were all but forgotten. I was entirely caught by surprise and I began to ask myself, "Why have I devoted so much of my energy and life currency (time) to starting this business?" This was certainly a huge adversity for me. I was to receive the greatest gift as a result however, and that is: "**Every adversity carries with it the seed of an equal or greater opportunity**", if you look. This idea completely changed my life. As we move through life, we can absolutely count on experiencing adversity. Our ability to quickly change our attitude is a key attribute for success. We call that having a high Adversity Quotient (AQ).

Fortunately, my feelings of disappointment passed in a week. I was beginning to develop my AQ, and began to look for a system that would bring us together as a cohesive unit with a common goal. After considering many management systems, I realized I was looking for something that offered much more. What I was seeking needed to include a way of bringing people together to create a positive business community with mutual goals for success. I looked at and evaluated many management systems, and felt that none of them fit the bill.

It was while attending a conference hosted by the Association of College Entrepreneurs in New York with Prof. John Chyzyk and a group of business students, that the system was to reveal itself. Retiring to my room after a hectic first day, I opened my conference package and found a little pea-green coloured book titled *Think and Grow Rich*, by Napoleon Hill. Two questions sprang to mind, "Who would ever publish a book using such a ridiculous colour?" and "Who would ever name their kid Napoleon?" I quickly stuffed the book back in the gift bag. Fairly soon I was to discover how naïve I was. I now blush in embarrassment at my reaction.

As I moved about the conference the next day, I discovered that Lee Iacocca, the man who had turned Chrysler around, and Michael Dell, the founder of Dell Computers, were among those who had used the principles contained in that pea-green book. When I returned to my room that night, I raced to my bed, grabbed that little book out of the bag and read it cover to cover that night. The more I read, the more I was convinced that Hill's ideas held the answers I was seeking to solve my corporate challenges. Not long after returning home, that same colleague invited me to attend the first Napoleon Hill Science of Success Instructor Training course to be given in Canada.

"Do you want to go?" Prof. Chyzyk asked. A quote from that little pea-green book came to mind, "Successful people make up their mind quickly and change it seldom," and so without hesitation I said, "Yes!" This relates to the idea that when the universe presents something, the timing or finances might not be ideal, however you need to act quickly. No procrastination!

While taking the Success Principles course, I had a sense that these principles would provide the positive change I was seeking. After completing my training, I created *The Science of Success* training program, set a location and time for the seminar in each region of Canada, and called together the franchisee offices in each province. Everyone was expected to attend, no exceptions. Some of the franchisees were outright hostile saying, "Who the heck do you think you are?" Regardless, I was armed with a system that I felt would make a positive impact on the business. I showed up at the specified seminar times, and so did they.

Each course was slated to run two full days plus an evening. I realized that, it would be challenging to carry off on my own. Who better to assist me than my personal coach, Vic Lindal, whose diverse skills and expertise made him the perfect choice for this adventure. Not only had he won numerous Toastmaster International speaking contests, he had also read Hill's book and used the principles in coaching award winning volleyball teams. I offered to train him in the principles in exchange for assistance in the task of training the franchisees. Without hesitation, Vic willingly joined me in this undertaking.

We conducted marathon training seminars consisting of more than 20 hours over two and a half days, in which the franchisees were taught the Success Principles. I told the franchisees they could bring their families, and noticed that extraordinary things began to happen. One franchisee came with her husband and teenage daughter. During a break, they went running into the hall and talked excitedly about the concept of a Major Definite Purpose and a Mastermind Alliance. Some franchisees brought their key staff members. A remarkable change took place in the company; the franchisees began to get excited and to share growing enthusiasm for the mission they were on. They began to adopt the Major Definite Purpose of making We Care the leading home healthcare company in Canada. In the ensuing years, we grew to 64 franchises, a remarkable accomplishment from our humble beginnings in our basement home office in the small city of Brandon, Manitoba. We became one of the largest home health care companies in Canada.

What was even more noteworthy was that all but one of the franchisees treated us like family, greeting us with hugs when we saw them. This one exception was a male British Army nurse who felt hugs weren't appropriate. Eventually, we were written up in a business magazine as being an exception in the franchise business world because our company demonstrated true mutual respect and camaraderie between the 64 franchisees and us, the franchisor.

D. Inoculating Kids for Success

Over time I noticed that the children of the franchisees who came with their parents to the success seminars were saying things like, "Why don't they teach things like this in the high schools?" They adopted the principles and were accomplishing remarkable goals. One 12-year-old daughter of a franchisee set the goal to join a ballet company, a challenging career to succeed in. Roughly ten years later, I received a call from this young lady who was passing through Brandon, MB on her way to a performance in Vancouver, BC. She had achieved her EndPoint Vision and was living the life she chose.

Of particular interest was Penny's experience, a franchisee from Medicine Hat, Alberta who had attended a seminar some years earlier with her daughter. This time she brought her son. They spent the weekend working together, discussing the principles and their application. He clarified his goal to win a golf tournament and become a golf pro at a major Canadian golf club. Not long after the seminar we received a wonderful email in which Penny excitedly described how her son had placed in the top three in one tournament and then subsequently won the next! Then she went on to say he had been offered the position of golf pro at a prestigious club in a large Canadian city!

Having four sons of my own, I wanted to inoculate them for success as well, and actually paid them to read that little pea-green book, *Think and Grow Rich*. As we progressed in the franchise training across the country, my sons participated in trainings, and in time contributed to the sessions. Their careers have flourished. I believe this early training strongly contributed to their success. Jeff and Rob became forensic psychiatrists, Jon an award winning financial investor, and Luke a successful musician, producer, singer and songwriter. The Success Principles apply to any field!

Seeing the sons and daughters of the franchisees finish the training and move on with an air of confidence, I found myself reflecting on my mother, who had been a marvelous athlete and could have achieved greatness in golf. Childhood worries and concerns as a young girl caring for her mother had ingrained in her ideas that were counter intuitive to achieving her dreams. I thought, if I could have trained her in these same Success Principles when she was a younger woman, it may have helped her live the life she wanted, by teaching her ways to dispel limiting beliefs. Thus, the idea of this book for children, parents and businesses was born.

As it turned out, the book also became an excellent training program for executives to learn the principles and how to use them in a business environment. Often, they would then make the leap, incorporating the principles into their families, allowing them to live a **congruent life**. That is, their approach to life could be the same at home as it was in the office.

E. Two Stories: Do Thoughts Create Reality?

1. The Bigger Bear

First, I would like to return to the concepts of the power of one's thoughts and the power of the law of attraction and manifestation. I had the idea of writing a book about an individual who had something significant to accomplish. While at my wilderness cottage, contemplating this book, I noticed a beaver swimming along the shore and became curious about their habits. I learned that the beaver is a family-oriented animal and until the age of two, the young beavers live at home and help to bring up the new kits. I also learned that at the age of two, the kits get kicked out of the home and must seek their own pond. It was then that the idea of *Possibility Pond* was born and the book began to take shape.

I decided to write the book in our guest camp located some distance from the main cottage. As I began to write, many times I wondered how a little two-year-old beaver would feel striking out from the safety of its home. One afternoon while returning to the cottage after taking a break in the local town, I noticed a small furry object on the side of the road. Getting out of the car to investigate I saw it was a young beaver with its little whiskers twitching fearfully at this large creature (me), that had come to examine him. We face many adversities in life, and it came home to me in that moment, that certainly for this beaver it must be a true adversity to seek out its own pond. Far from the safety of its family home, this young beaver must face many fears—being so vulnerable to predators such as bears, wolves, coyotes, eagles and owls. Life is about finding the opportunity behind the adversity. This expression rolled off my tongue so easily I thought, but what would I be thinking and feeling if I were in danger of being pursued by a bear? What kind of fear would this little beaver experience? I had no idea, but the universe would soon deliver an experience to help me understand more clearly.

Not long after having these thoughts I awoke in the middle of the night by the frightening sound of scratching on the side of the cottage. At this dark hour, the disembodied sound was terrifying. I forced myself to go out and investigate further. Stepping out of the safety of my cottage I came around the corner, there were the signs, fresh bear scat on the deck and claw marks on the side of the cottage. In the 25 years I had been coming to our cottage, nothing like this had ever happened. There were certainly bear on the property, but they tended to stay a respectful distance away. This was a new and different experience. Did my wish to understand the little beaver create this new reality?

This particular bear began to haunt the cottage regularly. After no success in having the bear removed, in an attempt to catch him, I baited the area to draw him back, but to no avail. Several sleepless nights passed without him showing up and it seemed the problem was solved. As soon as I stopped my all-night vigils the bear scat was deposited again. This continued until I had the idea to scratch the cedar shakes higher than he had done giving him the message that a bigger bear dominated this area. The idea worked. The bear stopped stalking the cottage and I gained understanding into the world of the beaver, and the fear he might have felt anticipating meeting a bear. Thank you Universe!

2. Determined Beavers

This second experience taught me that I had to be careful what I wished for, to be precise and be sure that it was truly what I wanted. As if I needed more convincing that the law of attraction and manifestation was indeed powerful, the universe provided yet another experience to bring the concept home. In the story of *Possibility Pond*, the expanding dimensions of the beaver pond were continually encroaching upon the access road to Farmer Ed's home and farm. One spring day, as Sandy and I came over the last rise before the lake, we slammed on the brakes in surprise to keep from careening into a new beaver pond. A dam had been built along the far side of the road from the pond and two feet of water now covered the road, making the cottage inaccessible.

It was surprising they had decided to back up the water in a small gully that seemed incapable of sustaining any beaver population! There were in my mind, many other places that the beavers could have chosen, and this particular location had never seemed to be of interest to them over the years.

Sandy and I looked at each other and started laughing. What came to life was a familiar saying, "**As you think, so shall you be.**" Another forceful example of, "You get what you think about, whether good or bad." Two hours later, after a lot of sweat and digging, the water had been lowered enough for us to make a dash across with the truck. It seemed to us that draining so much water would solve the problem, as this late in the summer there would not be enough water to support beavers and they would move on.

It is often said that beaver dams are the kidneys of the earth, filtering pollutants from the water. When we returned two weeks later, we found the beavers had been busy and nature's kidneys had been restored. The dam had been rebuilt, bigger, and better with more water backed up behind it. The universe really wanted us to get the lesson and now it was firmly etched in our minds. To solve the problem, we had to get a tractor in to dig a trench and put in a protected culvert to keep the area drained. Not only did we learn about the power of our thoughts, the beavers emphasized the lesson to achieve success: **Determination must be present.**

The beavers re-built the dam even bigger and stronger.

Laughter Makes the Journey Feel Shorter

The Irish say that laughter is a way to shorten the length of the road that you are travelling, especially if it is an arduous journey. As was my experience of finding a joyful carpentry mentor, Mr Martin Marion (see this story at the end of chapter 11).

Mr. Marion would approach tasks as both a challenge and a bit of fun, testing his ingenuity. It made our road to success feel shorter.

Another gift he gave me was his lack of envy for people who were more well off than him. He would say with his French Canadian accent, "The sun she shines on you, then the sun she's gonna shine on me." Jealousy was not in him. He believed he could create the life he loved (as Billy the Beaver did).

Some Ideas on Helping Keep the Earth Healthy (and ourselves)

As mentioned in the story, the two young beavers, Billy and Chewie, cut down many trees that end up floating away as the stream is too fast flowing to stop. Trees are the most wondrous and dependable beings on earth because they oxygenate the air we breathe, they are thought of as the lungs of the earth. It may seem terrible then, to see young beavers apparently destroying trees. However, there are a few points to consider. Beavers are said to be the kidney makers of the earth, as they create ponds in diverse terrains. The vegetation that grows in and around these new ponds acts to purify the water and support new life. The ponds are also helpful contributors to water management. Beavers prefer to eat poplar trees which create extensive root systems allowing them to regenerate rapidly after being cut. Nature works in a wondrously co-operative way. We think of the result as a micro-climate, it is cooler in the summer and, also attractive to wild life, increasing the health of the overall natural community. Also, the soil is prevented from running off into larger bodies of water, no longer silting them up, which if left unchecked leaves the soil less arable. After being wiped out centuries ago, **England has reintroduced the beaver** to their country to help rebuild the health of the environment. Their extinction was brought about by the country's desire for pelts to make hats, and scent glands to make perfume, medicine and whiskey. This unchecked hunting, combined with the lack of a long term vision resulted in destruction of the natural ecology in England. The steps being taken now are bringing life back to the wild places.

It is worth reflecting further on how nature can balance itself and how we can participate in this positive change. From 1914 to 1926 wolves were aggressively hunted in Yellowstone National Park in the U.S.A., because they were perceived as a pest and a threat to livestock. What followed was a cascade of disastrous changes to a balanced ecosystem. Elk, deer and coyotes began to over populate the park. Trees and land were over grazed, leading to a disappearance of beavers who could no longer build dams. This resulted in erosion, creating an inhospitable environment for plants, willow and aspen tree growth. The domino effect of eliminating wolves also lead to the loss of cold water fish, as without the shade of trees and plants water temperatures rose in rivers. These are just a few of the things that brought the Yellowstone ecosystem to its knees.

When wolves were reintroduced to the park, deer and elk populations were rebalanced, willow and aspen trees began to thrive and riverbanks were stabilized. Animals and birds that had left the park began to return, recreating a healthy eco system. This is one example of how we can proactively regenerate the planet. Further, 35 million dollars is generated yearly from wolf tourism in the park compared to the onetime cost of 30 million dollars to reintroduce them.

Today, many people, particularly younger generations, are alarmed and have been moved to action to help bring balance back to the environments that sustain us. One area of environmental concern is the unchecked clear cutting of so many forests around the world. Forests are a key system for our survival on this planet. Like the reintroduction of the wolves into Yellowstone, planting trees will act to bring back balance to the environment. The act of creating balance includes managing the needs of the forest ecosystems with the needs of humans. This is a delicate task requiring much diplomacy. The Success Principles presented in Possibility Pond, can increase the chances for successful change as it teaches **the skills needed to make positive choices** and exchanges with others. A mandate of balancing a sustainable harvest with regeneration of our forests can be done in an amenable fashion when we have the skills to work together.

It is said that if everyone in the world planted six trees in six years, a number of environmental challenges the world is now experiencing, would be greatly reduced. My wife and I have planted 88 trees on our city lot which is a little larger than the average lot size. This has helped to cleanse the air around us and we built a fence which holds the fresh oxygen and makes for more, local clean air. In this way, our family can enjoy more highly oxygenated clean air which is essential for good health. The wilding of our yard has provided a habitat for many pollinators such as the diverse bee population and, especially for the monarch butterfly which is endangered. As more families create diversity on their property, it creates a much larger forest, like a patch work quilt of many pieces and provides security for the future for nature and for us.

A final key take-away from Possibility Pond: Adventurizing

Billy's journey is meaningful to many people in numerous ways. His journey can be considered an adventure which is something we all should consider embarking on. When our grand-daughter Marlowe, was 8, she created the word 'Adventurizing.' She wrote this word in a card she gave to my wife and I for Christmas, stating, "I love you because you adventurize, are caring and love fun." There is no dictionary word, adventurize, however the root is adventure and we use her word regularly to describe how we live our life. Adventurizing is a key concept and one that may help us thrive in this rapidly changing and, seemingly dangerous, world. Let's explore this concept and its meaning further. Could Billy's journey be called an adventure? We believe that taking adventures is critical to everyone's well-being, young and old. However, this beautiful word, brought into existence by our granddaughter, applies to much more than taking a trip.

The dictionary definition of adventure is, "to engage in hazardous and exciting activity, especially the exploration of unknown territory." And what is "unknown territory?" Although we often think of a physical place that is unexplored or unfamiliar, it can also be unfamiliar knowledge, experience, or an activity. There are many more forms of adventurizing, such as reading a book, taking a course in a challenging area, meeting new people, travel, getting along with and managing people etc. Some of these adventure possibilities, such as meeting new people, might seem surprising. When meeting someone for the first time though, there is the risk of rejection, which could result in hurt feelings. Hazardous then? Yes. However, meeting people is an activity that is vital to pursue, as it is a key to longevity. Billy learned "to be a success, you must take others with you." He also learned the success principle Mastermind Alliance or MMA which requires the involvement of others in your journey to success. Other examples of adventurizing could be: learning to play a musical instrument, learning to sing, to act, learning a new sport. Please add to this list. The best advice we can offer to determine your path for adventurizing is given by Nike, "Just do it!" A modified quote by St Augustine dramatically emphasizes the importance of adventurizing, "The world is a book and those who do not adventure, read only one page." Hmmm, Billy concludes that a life without adventurizing is a life lacking interest or success.

Was Billy's journey an Adventure? We must respond with a resounding yes! In his case, he was often in physical danger travelling alone across unfamiliar lands where there are many predators such as wolves, bears, and owls who would love to eat him. Certainly, it qualifies as a risky and hazardous trip. Also, his decision to go to Impossible Creek, carried the additional risk that the whole beaver colony would think that there was something wrong with him and perhaps shun him, a cruel punishment. I often think of Dan Rather who said, "If all difficulties were known at the start of a long journey, most of us would never start out at all." Certainly, risk factors in any journey must be considered by you, but you must often proceed anyway. The biggest risk when we do not embrace adventurizing is missing out on the many choices that contribute to living a full life.

Billy's experience makes clear that the biggest dangers you, the reader, and I face are: We all have at this moment, an adventure bubble consisting of all the adventures that we are willing to take. Many start with a small bubble, slowly expanding it as they gain experience, knowledge and skills. Some people may have developed a good sized and healthy adventure bubble, but as they age, they shrink its size with more and more anti-adventurizing. The self-talk (by EGOR) such as "I am too old or too young to do that (whatever the adventure is) can limit us. Other examples: "I do not want to risk my health" or "I shouldn't spread myself too thin." This self-talk often begins when we are very young and stays with us as we grow up. Billy offers his wisdom to encourage you to build your best life, "**We adventurize, not to escape life, but for life to not escape us.**"

I recently watched a movie titled *Edie*, about an 83 year old woman who did not go on an adventure with her father when she was a young woman (thereby escaping life) and spends years being resentful and bitter, and not adventurizing. She voluntarily cares for a bitter and mean husband. When her husband dies, it becomes clear to her, that life could end at any time. She "wakes up" and decides that she wants to go on an adventure and climb the mountain her father had suggested so many years prior--a mountain she could have ascended with ease at a much earlier age. The journey forces her to overcome significant risk and challenge, and she ends up creating powerful memories for herself and gains vitality and joy. She enlarged her adventure bubble! She feels alive and now wants to Live Life to the Fullest. It is worth noting that watching a movie like this or, simply reading a good book, can bring the experience of adventurizing into your life creating a similar impact.

Billy story says to all readers, Adventurize! You will learn a lot about yourself, receive the best education ever and experience a fulfilling life. Having read this story, you now know important Success Principles and their application, and you are now inoculated for success.

Marlowe's advice has morphed into our Mission Statement: We will adventurize, living life in a caring, loving and mindful manner, full of gratitude, and we will have fun.

Acknowledgements

What I am sharing next is an example of a Mastermind Alliance, and describes a sample of some of the people and groups that assisted me on my journey. To be sure, there are many other whose names have not been mentioned, though they live on in my heart with gratitude.

As always, a project is brought to life by the work of many hands. I acknowledge and value the inspiration of Napoleon Hill Publications , and the Napoleon Hill Institute that maintains Hill's work, offering seminars and publications. They have greatly assisted me in my journey to create and live my best possible life. I give heartfelt thanks to the many people who have been an important part of my Mastermind Alliance over the years, in particular, Vic Lindal, Dan Doherty, and Sandy McMaster, who have always supported and assisted me in the realization of my vision. You cannot be a success without taking others with you.

Dan's publishing company is aptly named Reciprocity Publishing. A definition for reciprocity (a most beautiful success word), is the practice of exchanging things with others for mutual benefit. I offer a special thanks to Dan who always goes the extra mile in assisting me to get my ideas to the public, and for his constant kindness and encouragement.

I humbly acknowledge Dr. Viktor Frankl, who has been an important inspiration for my work and for Billy's optimism and faith when he visualized the building of a dam and the resulting home and pond. Frankl's book, *Man's Search for Meaning*, which was based on his experiences in several Nazi concentration camps during World War II. It has become one of the most influential books in the world and has been identified as one of the top 10 books ever written, the Bible being first on the list! He described how every morning, when he and other prisoners struggled out the door of their shelter, there was a selection process. Some were sent to the gas chambers to die, others to brutal work sites. He attributes his survival to his end-point vision, in which he daily visualized seeing himself lecturing in a classic lecture hall in Vienna. In exquisite detail, he would visualize the hall with beautiful seating, lighting, carpets … a total reality he created in his mind. He miraculously survived, when so many others did not, even when he was often too weak to perform his duties! I had the good fortune to speak with him on the phone for ¾ of an hour at his home in Vienna in 1997.

A personal success principle I practice is to always pass on a compliment. When presenting a class to the franchisees in our company, We Care Home Health Services, one of the attendees said, "Where do you get these amazing ideas", to which I replied, "from Viktor Frankl." At that point a compliment needed to be passed on so I asked my secretary to contact him. When I got him on speaker phone, I expressed my heartfelt gratitude to him for his inspirational book. I shared with him how it had made a significant and positive impact on our company, our several thousand employees across Canada, and to myself. He responded by saying, "Thank you. If I can do anything for you George, then please let me know." His words, to this day, have been a source of inspiration for me and one that can be adopted. In the character Billy, I encompassed many of the values that Viktor wrote about.

To My Four Sons Jeffry, Luke, Jon and Robert

Thank you for being open to these concepts and for taking the seminars (and teaching parts of them). Not only have you learned the Success Principle concepts you have come to embody them, living successful, fulfilling and loving lives. You provided the motivation to complete this work. I love all of you deeply.

Dr. Ralph Stanton

I would like to acknowledge Dr. Ralph Stanton, the founder of the Mathematics and Computer Science Faculty at the University of Waterloo, Waterloo, Ontario. Through his actions over many years he demonstrated how to be a great mentor, contributing to my success, and creating opportunities that allowed life to flow smoothly and productively. As a father of four boys, he provided me with a great model.

When I graduated from high school in the small Northern Ontario mining town of Kirkland lake, Dr. Stanton drove up from Waterloo and asked whether I would consider registering at the University of Waterloo. I felt honored, however what greatly impacted me was his statement, "If you continue to perform academically, I will always open doors for you," and he was true to his word and more. Funding in the form of scholarships, and other opportunities, were always forthcoming throughout my academic pursuits. Later, as my career took shape, Dr. Stanton provided job references and opened the door to academic positions. Many opportunities appeared and were supported by him throughout my career as he had promised. I also felt honored by his asking me to co-author the revised version of his text, Numerical Analysis for Science and Engineering, a Prentice Hall Publication.

Throughout my life, I have consciously endeavored to model Dr. Stanton's attitude and mentor approach with many young academics and entrepreneurs. Thank-you Ralph, your gift of mentorship continues to fill me with immense gratitude, as does the desire to emulate you. Dr. Stanton passed on April 21, 2010 at the age of 86.

Professor John Chyzyk

John was a colleague of mine at Brandon University. We were fellow academics who thrived on striving to help students become the best they could be. On one particular occasion we took a group of business students to New York City, to attend a conference on entrepreneurship. It was there that I first became acquainted with the Success Principles of Napoleon Hill. It was not long after returning from New York that John called me and said, "The first Napoleon Hill Instructor's course on Success Principles, is being given in Toronto, would you like to go?" Knowing that **Successful people make up their mind quickly and change it seldom**, I replied yes.

The course was life changing for myself and my co-founded corporation We Care Home Health Services and my family. I knew then that I had the ability to inoculate my children to be a success, and the ideas have guided my life from that point on. This book was certainly inspired and gifted by that learning. I am grateful that John had the vision and enthusiasm to get us to this course.

We attended many international conferences together where we jointly won best paper several times. This adventurizing also included participating in a fishing derby at Lake of the Woods in Canada every year for 26 years with a group of 18 friends. They were from diverse back- grounds, and this experience provided ideas that became inspiration for the story when describing how Billy interacted with his MMA.

I also learned from John, how to really connect with people, and that this is one of the most desirable attributes a person can possess. John gets my vote as the most positive person I have ever met. He freely says, "I Love Life" and is full of gratitude. Thank you John. You have truly been a life-long friend and motivator.

Jim McMaster

To my brother Jim, his adventurous spirit has shown me how to live life to the fullest. I am grateful we continue to adventurize together and create long lasting memories. Never at a loss for words, he often comes up with inspirational expressions to live by such as, "Go to solution, not problem". Thanks for being both brother and friend.

Sandy McMaster

I now acknowledge my life partner and express my deep gratitude to my wife Sandy McMaster, who believed in the vision of a book that taught Success Principles and enabled people to achieve their dreams. Sandy assisted in manifesting this book in the best possible way, cheering me along and professionally editing my work. As a Success Principle Instructor, guided visualization expert, and counsellor she was well versed in the concepts put forth in this book. She knows me so well, that she could readily transform my written thoughts while enhancing, clarifying and making eloquent what I wanted to express. Sandy exemplifies a person operating as a critical member of a Mastermind Alliance. Her positive attitude and willingness to go the extra mile are exemplary. This book, giving people a well-defined system to achieve their dreams, simply would not exist without her. With her love, support and belief, Possibility Pond has become the story I, and then we, envisioned. Also, our joint shared knowledge of Success Principles has made our marriage truly amazing. For these wonderful gifts, I am forever grateful.

And Finally

A lifetime of learning has taught me that we are never alone in our endevours. Though names may be missing, it is with deep gratitude that I thank the many people who have crossed my path, walked with me a ways and shared their gits and inspiration.

About the Creators

Author: George McMaster, Ph.D.

Dr. McMaster is currently professor emeritus at Brandon University. He has published numerous research papers in a variety of areas, many of them concerning the application of systems analysis and human resources to increase business productivity, for which he was awarded best paper at several international conferences. While an invited visiting scholar at Stanford University, Dr. McMaster was approached by Steve Jobs of Apple Computers to evaluate the productivity of the software division, which he successfully completed. This led to a job offer with Apple which he did not accept, choosing Canada and his academic career in the country he loved.

While teaching Computer Science at the University of Waterloo, Dr. McMaster was asked to join the team that subsequently founded Computer Science departments at York University in Ontario, the University of Manitoba, and Brandon University. He became a tenured faculty member at each of the institutions. While at the University of Manitoba, Dr. McMaster co-created an optical mark card for the Manitoba Department of Education that allowed software to be encoded quickly without the need for hardware. Millions of optical cards were used through-out the Manitoba high school Computer Science Program and the innovative copyrighted design concept was investigated by NASA as a productivity tool. During his tenure at Brandon University, Dr. McMaster received the Presidential Order of Merit for his professional work and service to enhance and advance the wider community. He was nominated by students for his classroom work which resulted in his receiving the Alumni Association Excellence in Teaching Award. He attributes the knowledge found in *Possibility Pond* for much of his success.

He co-founded We Care Home Health Services, growing the company to 64 franchises. During this time Dr. McMaster trained as and became, a *Science of Success* instructor, developing a training program for the company that helped secure its success as a leader in Canadian home healthcare. That same training program allowed him to go on to coach and train other corporations. Hotel Place Louis Riel in Winnipeg, Manitoba achieved the Best Medium Sized Business award following their team's participation in the training. He was sought after by the Thinking Expedition Corporation out of Houston, Texas, to participate in a program working with the Halliburton Corporation. He earned the title of Dr. Difffferent, due to his unique ability to innovate and inspire. Dr. McMaster attributes his zest for life and learning to his unquenchable curiosity.

George has four accomplished sons, Jeffry, Luke, Jonathon and Robert. He attributes their success in part, to their knowledge of the material in *Possibility Pond*, and *EndPoint Vision and Beyond*, a book cowritten with Master Coach, Vic Lindal. George and his wife, Sandy, live on their pollinator friendly property in Ontario.

While at the University of Manitoba, Dr. McMaster was asked to deliver a 13 week course, three hours a week, to students at Brandon University as a first step to the creation of their Computer Science Program. This was an exciting opportunity, and as a private pilot, he was able to fly himself back and forth between Brandon and Winnipeg to teach the course, saving time and allowing him to fulfill his teaching requirements at the University of Manitoba. Dr. McMaster's love of flying expanded with the introduction of ultralite planes to the aviation world. He eventually built his own, (with flying specs of plus 5 G's and minus 2 G's), as the pleasure of "Slipping the surly bonds of earth and dancing the skies on laughter silvered wings" appealed greatly to him.

His wife Sandy has been a yoga practitioner for many years, which motivated McMaster to suggest going to India for training, and as a means of learning more about her love of the practice. They went to Rishikish in India to attend a six week life-changing course, becoming certified Yoga instructors. They share this nature of curiosity which fuels many of the quests they have been on.

The Adventurizing article in the latter pages of this book give more details about the author's lifestyle. It stresses the importance for all of us to set the intention to adventurize, for our health, for living life to the fullest, and for having few regrets.

The definitions for intent are critical: "having or indicating an efficient, practical and systematic approach to a task", "determination or motivation (to do something)", and "a perseverance or industry in carrying out a task or action." Dr. McMaster set the intent to adventurize at a very young age and these adventurizing ideas are shared in an effort to inspire the reader to find their own adventure to partake in. Currently, he is taking an advanced, intensive seminar by Dr. Joe Dispenza with his wife, on the way to being healthier, both physically and mentally, and being able to manifest a life that they love.

Artist: Albert Casson

Albert Casson is a professional wildlife, landscape and portrait artist, who infuses his pieces with passion and vitality. Casson specializes in detailed drawings, paintings, and illustrations. He is a natural artistic genius with a pedigree that includes A.J. Casson of the Group of Seven. He has been commissioned by Kodak Canada, Panasonic Canada, Royal City Realty, Guelph, Molson Indy, the Calgary Zoo, the Vancouver Aquarium and others. He provides incentive and gift ideas from concept to product completion and promotion. He is also the founder and instructor for the Casson School of Art where he endeavours to inspire others to follow their path of creativity.

When approached by Dr. McMaster to create the art for *Possibility Pond*, Casson was excited by the opportunity to contribute to the project. He resonated with the story and preliminary sketches. He was inspired by Billy Beaver and his Mastermind Alliance, particularly connecting with Elder. Casson's enthusiasm for the book and his exceptional talent have truly brought the characters and principles to life.

Editor: Sandy McMaster, M.Ed.

Sandy worked as a therapist with youth and adults for 20 years. She is also a successful artist, author, editor, and yoga teacher. Sandy is co-editor and contributing author of *Dancing on the Earth: Women's Stories of Healing Through Dance* and editor for *Possibility Pond* and *EndPoint Vision and Beyond*. Sandy believes in the power of visioning to create the life you wish. She recently created workshops using the ancient form of the mandala. She uses guided visualization and other forms of expressive arts to help individuals find their true path. Sandy became a *Science of Success* Instructor and delivered Success Principles seminars with her husband Dr. George McMaster for over a decade. Sandy believes in her husband's vision to make Success Principles accessible to all, and is grateful to be part of his Mastermind Alliance

Designer/Publisher: Daniel Doherty, M.A.

Dan is always looking for processes that get results. His passion is integrating adult education, communication technology and group process. As a publisher he facilitates people's stories and valuable ideas into public awareness. As an educator, he recognizes how Dr. McMasters' storytelling and education skills adapt the Success Principles in a way that people can learn from and apply them, personally and at work. By incorporating Dr. McMasters' inspiring story and Mr. Casson's delightful artwork, he believes this book of Napoleon Hills' Success Principles will serve generations of aspiring souls who seek to make a positive difference in their lives and the lives of others.

This is the third book Dr. McMaster and Dan have collaborated on. The others being: *Radical Coaching* and *EndPoint Vision and Beyond*. Dan adapted *EndPoint Vision* into a workshop, e-course, AI coaching app and life planning game. These are available from www.endpointvision.com

Success Principle Checklist/Log

Here is a quick-review checklist you can use to log your results from using the Success Principles.

1. **Major Definite Purpose (MDP)**: Identify something significant yet to do.	
2. **Mastermind Alliance (MMA)**: Bring at least one person with you.	
3. **Faith (F!)**: Believe your MDP will happen.	
4. **Go the Extra Mile (GEM)**: Give service when none is expected.	
5. **Personal Initiative (PI)**: Reach out; ask a stranger.	
6. **Pleasing Personality (PP)**: Make a pleasing gesture; be generous.	
7. **Positive Mental Attitude (PMA)**: The mind works better with positivity + action.	
8. **Enthusiasm (E!)**: Bring eager enjoyment and interest.	
9. **Self-Discipline (SD)**: If it is to be it is up to me.	
10. **Accurate Thinking (AT)**: Be skeptical, focus on facts, verify sources.	
11. **Controlled Attention (CA)**: Bring purpose and focus to your actions.	
12. **Teamwork (T!)**: **T**ogether **E**ach **A**chieves **M**ore	
13. **Learning from Adversity and Defeat (LADD)**: In the middle of difficulty lies opportunity. Look for it.	
14. **Creative Thinking (CT)**: Look for ideas. Entertain unusual perspectives.	
15. **Budget Time and Money (BTM)**: Time-box strategic activities and monitor money.	
16. **Health (H!)**: Eat food that has life force in it. Avoid drugs, processed food and sugar. Sleep well.	
17. **Cosmic Habit Force (CHF)**: Work with the influence of the cosmos.	
18. **Determination (D!)**: Never give up. Be a dog with a bone.	
19. **Persistence (P!)**: Continue despite difficulty or opposition	
20. **Adaptability to Change (A2C)**: Accept what is and keep your eyes open for opportunity.	

Possibility Pond

www.ingramcontent.com/pod-product-compliance
Lightning Source LLC
Chambersburg PA
CBHW050503110426
42742CB00018B/3349